No Ways Tired:
The Public Historically Black College Dilemma

Kyra M. Grimes-Robinson

Against the Grain Communications
Clayton, OH

Earlier, unpublished versions: *State-Mandated Integration and Public Historically Black Colleges and Universities: A Study of Public Relations Strategies and Plans* © 1995; *The Journey of Public Historically Black Colleges (HBCUs): Adversity, Rebirth, and Survival into the 21st Century* © 1997

If you would like to express any comments or questions or would like to request additional copies of *No Ways Tired*, please email the author at CKROB7071@aol.com, write to Against the Grain Communications, P.O. Box 58, Clayton, Ohio, 45315, or visit the 1st Books website at www.1stbooks.com.

Visit our web site at: http://www.ckellyrobinson.com/

Printed in the United States of America

ISBN 1-58500-563-0

Library of Congress Catalog Card Number: 99-95520

1stbooks - rev.01/27/00

Nurturing. Cultivating. Inspiring. Uplifting. Resilient. Enlightening. Encouraging. Struggle. Progress. These are but a few descriptors that capture the very essence of an entity that has touched and empowered a people for over 150 years. While small in number (109), HBCUs (Historically Black Colleges and Universities) are mighty forces and beacons of hope and educational access.

The "HBCU Experience" can be found at Howard, Fisk, Mississippi Valley State, Morehouse, Tougaloo, and Shaw, to name a few. Simply put, these legacies have left an indelible mark on the educational history of African Americans. These institutions are to be cherished and revered forever--or lost as the 21st century approaches. Threatened daily by internal and external forces, HBCUs are fighting one of their toughest battles ever.

Cover Credit: I would like to thank the following family members and friends, all of whom are HBCU alumni, for allowing their commencement pictures to grace the cover of this work: Vedette A. Woods-Ecton (Central State University); Donna Bostic-Ward, Chester K. Robinson (Howard University); Yul K. Amerson (Harris-Stowe State College); Kyra M. Grimes-Robinson, Tiffany L. Bridgewater (Fisk University); Russell K. Robinson (Hampton University); and Dionne Lomax, Gisele Ransom-Garraway (Howard University). NOTE: Harris-Stowe State College graduation picture of Yul K. Amerson, courtesy of Joelle and John McIntosh. *About the Author* photograph, courtesy of Dr. Eileen O'Brien.

To my husband, Chet, and my mother, Janice, thank you for being my rock, support and encouragement as I pursued this endeavor. Your unconditional love, faith and prayers have been my sustenance.

Interview Sources

The following respondents have granted permission to use their responses:

Donald K. Anthony

Mark Anthony

Deirdre Baldwin*

Kimberly Bunton-Douglas

Michele Coleman

Angela M. Dixon

Rochelle Neal*

Ralph L. Payne

Kathy O. Peale

Lawrence E. Porter

Phyllis Qualls-Brooks

Robert L. Smith

Marcus Walker*

Margaret C. Whitfield

Wanda R. Young

*Denotes that names are fictitious and have been modified.

Table of Contents

List of Tables

When I embarked upon this endeavor several years ago, I never realized the impact that it would have on me, much less the significance it could have to others. However, the critical nature of this project became all the more evident to me when I began researching and sharing my discoveries with others. I was deeply appalled and disturbed to find that many, especially African Americans, were unaware about the integration demands that have been placed upon HBCUs and the constant threats of mergers and closure. Further, they were also ill-informed about the legal cases which have engulfed these entities for decades. And, not surprisingly, some academicians in the mainstream realm of higher education were also ignorant about HBCUs, their struggles, and integration's impact on these institutions. At this moment, I realized that I must pursue this project wholeheartedly in an attempt to inform the public about the historical, social, and academic significance of these treasures and their daily fight for survival.

Even more recently, I have witnessed first-hand the lack of knowledge that others have about HBCUs. Having been an employee of Harris-Stowe State College, a St. Louis historically black college, I was afforded the opportunity to share my expertise on this subject with my colleagues. Much to my surprise, many of them did not know about the integration legal battles of our sister institutions in neighboring states. They simply did not realize how close this matter hit home, as the only other Missouri HBCU, Lincoln University, has experienced a significant decrease in its African-American student body and faculty over the last few years. Furthermore, as a native of Dayton, Ohio and a graduate of Fisk University (located approximately a mile from Tennessee State University), I have watched closely as the Central State University and Tennessee State University situations have unfolded. When I completed my interviews in 1995, I had no idea that this project would foreshadow what was to transpire over the next few years. African Americans have become complacent, ignoring the signs around them. More often than not, there is little or no regard or respect for these entities in their surrounding communities, let alone in mainstream American higher education.

Initially, I too, accepted the "status quo." I was not convinced this work could make a difference and even wrestled with whether or not I should pursue publication. However, my revelation appeared in April 1997, when I attended the 22nd Annual NAFEO Conference in Washington D.C. Attending the sessions "Historically Black Colleges and Universities: Keeping the Doors of Opportunity Open" and "Keeping Open the Doors to Equal Educational Opportunity: A Forum Sponsored Jointly by NAFEO, the National Black Caucus of State Legislators and the National Bar Association" renewed my heartfelt interest in this matter. As a graduate of a private black university and a former employee of Harris-Stowe State College, I have a vested interest in these institutions. If I can contribute to the HBCU knowledge base, then I must do so. Educators and the masses -- general public -- can benefit and learn from *No Ways Tired: The Public Historically Black College Dilemma.*

The pages which follow present but a glimpse of HBCUs, exploring and evaluating HBCUs' origins, legal battles, financial status, and survival strategies. Yet, while it is important to understand the past, it is equally critical to appreciate the present and prepare for the future. The interviewees shared their innermost thoughts, feelings, and passion about HBCUs. While doing so, they provided an understanding of the administrative, alumni, and student perspective.

Without their assistance, cooperation and candor, *No Ways Tired* would have only been an aspiration. I thank all of you for the opportunity to talk with you.

Even more important, I would like to thank others who, perhaps unbeknownst to them, contributed to this work. First and foremost, I would like to thank my Lord and Savior Jesus Christ, in whom "I can do all things." Second, I am grateful for my family, friends, and Harris-Stowe colleagues who encouraged me to press on and pursue this. Third, four of my professors, Dr. L.M. Collins of Fisk University; Dr. Eddith Dashiell, Dr. Hugh Culbertson, and Dr. Cassandra Reese (all of Ohio University), strengthened my writing abilities in ways that are immeasurable. Fourth, I praise Fisk for cultivating my love for HBCUs. Last, and certainly not least, I would like to show my gratitude to two well-renowned Fisk alumni, Nikki Giovanni and Dr. John Hope Franklin, and Tom Joyner, host of the nationally syndicated radio program *The Tom Joyner Morning Show* and an alumnus of Tuskegee University. Ms. Giovanni, Dr. Franklin, and Mr. Joyner responded to my plea for assistance in pursuing a work of this nature and reiterated its value and worth. You replied when others with your standing and honor in the African–American community would not. Thanks again to everyone and may God continue to bestow many blessings upon all of you.

Chapter One
A Brief Glimpse of the Pressing Issue at Hand

Nurturing. Cultivating. Inspiring. Uplifting. Resilient. Enlightening. Encouraging. These descriptors capture the very essence of entities that have empowered a people for over 150 years. Historically black colleges and universities (HBCUs) are beacons of hope and educational opportunity. These institutions embody African-American strife and triumphs, and are reminders that education has always been a motivating and sustaining force for African Americans. Even during slavery, many slaves secretly learned to read and write. Yet, as an integral part of the African-American experience, education has meant more than mastering basic reading, writing, and mathematical skills. To many African Americans, education has symbolized not only economic and social empowerment but also success and equality. Without an education, peoples of African descent would be positioning themselves for failure and a hopeless future.

This desire for educational access and opportunity was the foundation of higher education for African Americans in this country. Before the Civil War, the earliest paradigms of higher education for African Americans were established. These historically black colleges and universities were Pennsylvania's Cheyney University, 1837; Lincoln University, 1854; and Ohio's Wilberforce University, 1856. These institutions and those which followed provided a formal education for ex-slaves and free blacks. For over a century and a half, HBCUs have been a permanent structure for the cultivation of African Americans. The "HBCU Experience," as it is often dubbed, can be discovered at Howard, Fisk, Mississippi Valley, Alabama A&M, Tougaloo, and Shaw, among others. These legacies have left an indelible mark on the academic history of African Americans. Institutions to be cherished and revered forever -- or lost as the 21st century approaches. Threatened daily by internal and external forces, HBCUs are confronting one of their toughest battles ever. Indeed, their struggle for survival, especially for public black colleges, continues.

During their existence, most of the remaining 109 HBCUs♦, which make up only 3 percent of American institutions of higher education, have encountered numerous difficulties -- especially financial -- at one time or another (Roebuck and Murty 103). *See Appendix A for a listing of all four-year HBCUs and their locations.* In spite of these problems, many have endured. Nonetheless, this triumph has been short-lived for many of the 50 public HBCUs, which in 1991, "enrolled about 71.4 percent of students at all HBCUs" (Briggs and Robinson 27). Today, their battle must be waged on all sides -- against internal and external opposition. Many critics have questioned the need for HBCUs, especially since they were established prior to the landmark case, *Brown v. Board of Education* (1954). Although met with resistance, African Americans were granted legal and civil rights to attend predominantly white colleges and universities after *Brown*. Therefore, critics say public HBCUs perpetuate segregation and believe the continued existence of HBCUs "provide a two-tiered higher education system within an integrated society, which is counterproductive financially, philosophically, and pedagogically" (Roebuck and Murty, Preface xi).

Perhaps just as damaging to the image and credentials of black colleges and universities, is the belief held by many, including some African Americans, that these institutions are academically inferior simply because they are predominantly black. Hare refutes these notions by contending that there are differing objectives for desegregation and effective education. While the first serves to provide better educational opportunities for minority students through exposure to diverse faculty and students, the latter emphasizes "increased academic outcomes and a decrease in the traditional attainment across groups" (212). Although Hare believes that the ideal model for educational institutions is effective desegregated schools, where diversity and academic effectiveness for all racial backgrounds coexist, his most compelling argument is that it is unfair to associate academic superiority with predominantly white schools and academic inferiority with predominantly African-American schools:

> It has been assumed . . . that all majority schools can be, and frequently are, effective although segregated, but that all minority schools are ineffective by definition. The drive for desegregation which labeled separate facilities for minorities as 'inherently unequal'. . . implicitly led us to assume that effective education for minorities was impossible without desegregation. (219-220)

Disagreeing with critics, HBCU advocates say HBCUs are needed because they provide not only an educational opportunity in a nurturing environment for African Americans who may not attend college otherwise, but also instill leadership characteristics and pride in the students' cultural heritage. Throughout matriculation, students are exposed to an *in loco parentis* environment, in which the staff and faculty serve as substitute parents who are supportive and want nothing less than the best for these students. Because of this team effort and unity, there is a holistic approach to academic learning and experiencing life. Furthermore, the central mission of HBCUs has always been and still is to take socioeconomically and academically disadvantaged youth and transform them into success stories -- leaders in education, politics, business, and the community. According to Barthelemy, "One of the advantages black colleges seem to have over the predominantly white schools is that they do more than educate their students; a spirit of leadership responsibility pervades the black campus" (19).

Often times, an underlying factor to the aforementioned dissension and differing opinions is the result of economics -- an unequal distribution of funds between the public white institutions and the public black institutions, which often lag behind in terms of financial resources and facilities. This situation has become a matter of the haves (the predominantly white colleges and universities) versus the have nots (the HBCUs). There have been attempted legal resolutions to this problem, as in *Brown v. Board of Education* (1954) and *U.S. v. Fordice* (1992). As a result, state court systems have threatened to either merge HBCUs with nearby predominantly white institutions or close them down completely. The fate of these schools is pending on court decisions. Mississippi has been watched closely, as HBCU advocates and administrators have monitored *U.S. v. Fordice*. This case is expected to set a precedent, compelling other states with public HBCUs to follow suit (Mercer, "Marching" A28).

Balancing the traditional educational missions of these institutions with the need for diversity has not been easy; it has been a dilemma for many administrators, faculty, alumni, and students. According to James Lyons, former president of Jackson State University:

> The dilemma is that we cannot argue that white institutions should develop affirmative action plans and diversify and then come back and still have HBCUs not do this. I believe that there's nothing wrong with singing *Lift Every Voice and Sing* [sic.] and *The Star Spangled Banner* [sic.]. My problem as the president of

an HBCU is that I don't want to have to stop singing *Lift Every Voice* [sic.]. (Briggs and Robinson 28-29)

Lyons makes a powerful and accurate assessment, one that expounds on the feelings of present and future alumni. To many alumni, the ultimate effects of diversity will be difficult to accept. On the one hand, they view their institutions as having always opened their doors to the masses. Exclusivity, as enforced by many of the majority institutions, has never been tolerated. Rather, inclusiveness is embraced. Yet, at the same time, alumni can not fathom revisiting their alma maters and seeing them as different entities -- HBCUs only in name and history, but not reflected in the colleges' student bodies, faculties, and administrations. A change of this magnitude represents the eradication and extinction of treasures that will be lost to their children and generations to come. Even so, for many African-American alumni of black colleges, this is becoming a bitter and harsh reality.

In this day, it is increasingly apparent that integration has and continues to influence the social, political, economic, and educational fabric of America. Because all of these facets are intertwined, the major emphasis of this book will explore integration in the higher education context and how social interaction, legal/political intervention, and economic realities shape the structure of black colleges and universities. Integration impacts all HBCU administrators, alumni, and students. These advocates are attempting to preserve HBCUs' identity while simultaneously incorporating diversity. Public relations is often one of the most significant tools used to help ease and alleviate alumni, student body, and faculty's feelings of hopelessness and anger triggered by states' integration demands. Yet, it remains to be seen if these public relations plans are working. Is public relations aiding in the transition? Can it be instrumental in developing effective survival strategies?

In an attempt to answer these questions and grasp how HBCUs arrived at their present status, there must first be an understanding of their origins, legal defeats and victories, and financial standing. Perhaps even more important, HBCU employees, graduates and students can provide the most revealing and realistic responses and solutions. This book examines all of the aforementioned perspectives. From January through March 1995, nine face-to-face and six phone interviews were conducted with staff members/representatives from University Relations (Public Relations/Public Information), Alumni Affairs/Relations, and Student Government Associations at the following public black institutions: Central State University, Tennessee State University, Kentucky State University, Alcorn State University, Mississippi Valley State University, and Jackson State University. At least one department/respondent was interviewed from each school. Asterisks denote fictitious names. The integrative stages at these universities run the gamut from not yet being state-mandated to integrate to having met state-mandated integration goals.

The open-ended questions gauged the public HBCUs' stance on integration and efforts to make changes, university representatives' opinions of HBCUs in general, and provided information on the number of graduates, predominant majors of graduates and the approximate ethnic background of faculties and student bodies. Most of the questions were posed to all interviewees, while others were tailored to specific schools and departments. These interviews, in one way or another, provided answers to the following questions:

- Do HBCUs serve a significant purpose economically, culturally, educationally, and socially?
- Is there truly a difference between integration and desegregation?

3

- Will it be possible for HBCUs to preserve their cultural heritage if forced to integrate and incorporate another culture's viewpoint and history?
- Does it appear that HBCU supporters -- administrators, alumni, and students -- advocate integration and the use of quotas in some cases (predominantly white universities), yet oppose them when applied to HBCUs? Why or why not?
- How are HBCUs coping with the possibility of closure or integration? What role does university public relations play in targeting those publics (alumni and students) who ultimately must deal with these issues?
- What public relations efforts have been used in recruiting and retaining other race students?

The outcomes of these interviews, compiled as case studies of each university, reveal not only a commitment to diversity, but also the sentiment and passion revolving around preserving the HBCU heritage and enhancing HBCUs' image. It is evident that these universities refuse to allow diversity to engulf and swallow the black college legacy and history.

The fears and concerns expressed in the interviews are not unfounded or absurd notions. They have been commonplace for years. In fact, Haynes, in his 1975 analysis of desegregation effects on 34 public black institutions, foreshadowed much of what has continued to happen over the last couple of decades. Interviewing chief executive administrators (presidents and vice-presidents), Haynes concluded that desegregation demands would place chief administrators and their institutions in awkward and paradoxical situations. Desegregation would force them to struggle with diversifying while maintaining HBCUs' cultural heritage and educational, social, and political commitment to the African-American community:

> The commitment to equal educational attainment and an integrated society has long been supported by the public black college. However, the position they occupy now suggests that, if the national policy on integration is fully applied to them, their importance as critical institutions in the black community will be jeopardized. (13-14)

In essence, these administrators wrestled with the same issues their present colleagues are facing, including recruitment of non-black faculty and students, continued existence based upon financial support from state and federal governments, and ensuring their heritage will not be diminished by integration (126, 144, 174). Nearly twenty-five years ago, these HBCU officials predicted that desegregation's most visible impact would be observed in the student bodies. They believed there would be an influx of non-black students, but black colleges and universities would continue to serve primarily African-American students. Also, alumni would demand greater involvement in the institutional policy-making (135-137, 141). Ironically, these visions have come to pass and HBCU administrators, alumni, and students find themselves in the difficult position of reconciling integrationist philosophy with Afrocentric philosophy and the strong need to cling to culture, history and pride.

♦It should be noted that it is very difficult to obtain an accurate account of HBCUs, as the number ranges from 103 to 117 in different sources. For purposes here, 109 will be used, as it was documented and seen the most often during research.

References

Books

Barthelemy, Sidney. "The Role of Black Colleges in Nurturing Leadership." *Black Colleges and Universities: Challenges for the Future*. Ed. Antoine Garibaldi. New York: Praeger Publishers, 1984. 14-25.

Hare, Bruce R. "Toward Effective Desegregated Schools." *College in Black and White: African American Students in Predominantly White and in Historically Black Public Universities*. Eds. Walter R. Allen, Edgar G. Epps, and Nesha Z. Haniff. Albany, NY: State University of New York Press, 1991. 211-223.

Haynes, Leonard L., III. "An Analysis of the Effects of Desegregation Upon Public Black Colleges." Dissertation. The Ohio State University, 1975.

Roebuck, Julian B., and Komanduri S. Murty. *Historically Black Colleges and Universities: Their Place in American Higher Education*. Westport, CT: Praeger Publishers, 1993.

Periodicals

Briggs, Jimmie, and Lori S. Robinson. "Black Colleges Under Fire." *Emerge* Sept. 1993: 26-31.

Mercer, Joye. "Marching to Save Black Colleges." *The Chronicle of Higher Education* 11 May 1994: A28, A31.

Established during the middle to late 1800s, mainly in the South and Northeast, HBCUs provided the first opportunity for many former slaves and others of African-American descent to receive a formal education. Many of these schools (especially the private ones) began as elementary and secondary schools and were later elevated to university status. The original purpose of these institutions was to educate and produce teachers, ministers, skilled and technical workers, and other community, political, and civic leaders in the African-American community. Defining HBCUs, Roebuck and Murty state:

> Historically black colleges and universities (HBCUs) are black academic institutions established prior to 1964 whose principal mission was, and still is, the education of black Americans. . . . They were originally established when segregation was mandated and now continue with predominately black enrollments on a voluntary basis. (3, 4)

In addition, these institutions, like their historically white counterparts, must be accredited by a national accrediting body or working towards accreditation. And, it should be noted that there is a difference between historically black and predominantly black institutions. While historically black universities are defined above, predominantly black institutions are those schools founded after 1964 and whose student body compositions are at least 50 percent black. For example, some of these schools are located in cities with large African-American populations -- New York, Detroit, and Chicago (Garibaldi 4).

The role of HBCUs is to do more than just educate students academically, for they also foster an environment in which there is self-cultivation, development, and edification. This is unique to the educational mission of HBCUs and often is not available to African-American students in other academic settings, as noted by Roebuck and Murty: "HBCUs, unlike other colleges are united in a mission to meet the educational and emotional needs of black students. . . . They provide an African-American culture and ambiance that many students find essential to their social functioning and mental health" (10, 17).

Providing additional support for this stance, Davis researched the differences between interpersonal relationships and networking/social support systems on black and white campuses, and whether these factors have a positive or negative impact on a student's academic success, academic life satisfaction, and career outlook. Surveying 888 black HBCU and 695 black students at historically white colleges, Davis hypothesized that: (1) HBCU students are more involved in extracurricular activities and have more access to social support networks, thereby attributing to fewer academic adjustment problems, (2) at black and white schools, students who use these support systems would probably have better GPAs and, (3) black students at HBCUs who utilize support systems will be more satisfied with their overall academic experience and have more challenging career goals (145-148). Even though Davis' results were inconclusive for the second hypothesis, he did find that black students were active on both black and white campuses, with HBCU students being more active (148-149). Likewise, interpersonal relationships among faculty/staff/students were positively correlated to college satisfaction on black and white campuses. But, black students attending white colleges had fewer support networks to choose from. With more access to networks, HBCU students were more integrated into the college environment and more satisfied with the college experience: "On Black [sic.] campuses, Black [sic.] students are exposed to caring and supportive institutional settings that foster psychological well-being and the positive direction necessary for learning" (157).

HBCUs, like many other institutional entities, have undergone numerous transformations that have revolutionized not only their history, but also that of African-American higher education as a whole. These various stages include the Torchbearer/Pre-Civil War Era (1837-1861), the Post-Civil War/Land Grant Era (1865-1895), the "Separate, But Equal"/Segregation Era (1896-1953), and the Desegregation/Public HBCU Integration Era (1954-present). Not surprisingly, these changes coincided with monumental historical events. The latter two eras are explained in more detail in Chapter Four, where they are defined through legal cases.

During the Torchbearer/Pre-Civil War Era, instructional facilities and resources for African Americans were scarce, thereby leaving many slaves to either teach themselves or rely on the help of altruistic Caucasians. Although there were some schools during this time, the earliest HBCUs -- Cheyney, Lincoln, and Wilberforce -- were the first postsecondary institutions for African Americans. Following the Civil War, more colleges and universities were organized with the assistance of the Freedmen's Bureau, an organization created by the federal government to provide educational, economic, medical, and legal assistance to former slaves; African-American religious denominations, and missionary societies, namely the American Missionary Association. Most of these were private, liberal arts schools. At the same time, many public HBCUs were founded as industrial, mechanical, or agricultural schools. These schools were organized because of the Second Morrill (Land Grant) Act of 1890, in which the federal government provided funding for these institutions (Roebuck and Murty 26-27).

Land Grant Acts of 1862 and 1890

Named for their creator, U.S. Congressman Justin Smith Morrill of Vermont, the Land Grant Acts (Morrill Acts) of 1862 and 1890 helped establish 17 land grant historically black colleges and universities. The first of these institutions was Mississippi's Alcorn State University, founded in 1871. Other universities soon followed, including Alabama A&M University (1875), Kentucky State University (1886), Florida A&M University (1887), North Carolina A&T University (1891), and Tennessee A&I (State) University (1912) (Walther 14-16, 25). The A's, M's, T's, and I's in the names of these institutions signified that agricultural, mechanical, technological, and industrial instruction were a major part of the curriculum.

The first Land Grant Act, passed on July 2, 1862, granted public land to several states and territories that would be used specifically for colleges specializing in the agricultural and mechanical sciences. Each state was to receive 30,000 acres of land for each representative and senator in Congress, according to their representation in the 1860 census (503). Perhaps the most important part of this legislation was expressed in Section 4, which stated that each state under the provisions of this act must support and maintain:

> At least one college where the leading object shall be, without excluding other scientific and classical studies, and including military tactics, to teach such branches of learning as are related to agriculture and the mechanic arts, . . . in order to promote the liberal and practical education of the industrial classes in the

several pursuits and professions in life. (504)

Further, the federal money given to these states was restricted in that it could not be used to buy, renovate or construct buildings (504).

On August 30, 1890, the Second Morrill Act was passed, having a more profound influence on the development of black land grant institutions. With the establishment of these public schools, blacks were to be given equal access to an industrial, mechanical, and agricultural education. More specifically, the Land Grant Act of 1890 was an intimation of what was to come -- "separate, but equal" educational facilities. That is, separate schools were organized for black and white students and federal dollars were to be distributed equally among all of these institutions:

> Provided that no money shall be paid out under this act to any State or Territory for the support and maintenance of a college where a distinction of race or color is made in the admission of students, but the establishment and maintenance of such colleges separately for white and colored students shall be held to be a compliance with the provisions of this act if the funds received in such State or Territory be equitably divided as hereinafter set forth. . . . The legislature of such State may propose and report to the Secretary of the Interior a just and equitable division of the fund to be received under this act between one college for white students and one institution for colored students . . . and thereupon such institution for colored students shall be entitled to the benefits of this act and subject to its provisions. (418)

According to Walther, the Land Grant Acts contributed to three important changes in higher education. First, the focus was now on vocational and technical education. Second, the American system of education was transformed from one which catered to the elite to one which served the masses. Third, new knowledge was produced as people accepted vocational education as a legitimate and feasible alternative to a classical and liberal arts education (34-35). As the education of blacks progressed during this period, two types of education emerged -- professional/vocational education and liberal arts education. Most of the black public institutions emphasized vocational education; whereas, the private schools focused on liberal arts. Eventually, both schools of thought became part of the foundation of African-American higher education, as seen in today's HBCUs: "On the conceptual level, anyway, black colleges believe in a liberal arts education, but they also insist on the utility of the liberal arts and do not fear to combine them with career education" (Kannerstein 47). In the late 1800s and early 1900s, these two philosophies divided the African-American community and educational system. The advocates for these ideologies were Booker T. Washington and W.E.B. DuBois.

The Great Debate -- Vocational Education or Liberal Arts Education?

Booker T. Washington, a graduate of Hampton Institute in Hampton, Virginia (now known as Hampton University, a private black university) and the founder of Tuskegee, Alabama's Tuskegee University (also a private HBCU), was the spokesperson for industrial/vocational education. Although this was not Washington's original concept, his own modification of industrial education has left an indelible mark on the educational history of African Americans. While a student at Hampton, Washington began to endorse the doctrine of Hampton's founder,

Samuel Chapman Armstrong, who believed in the value of buying property and homes, and of learning vocations and trade skills. Washington made these ideas his platform and philosophy on life for African Americans. The only way for African Americans to achieve success and the respect of white America -- especially the Southern Aristocracy -- was through economic empowerment, made possible through acquiring skills and providing those services the world wanted and needed (Franklin and Moss 244-245). African Americans could lift themselves up and strengthen their communities, for he once said, "I plead for industrial education and development for the Negro not because I want to cramp him, but because I want to free him. I want to see him enter the all-powerful business and commercial world" (qtd. in Franklin and Moss 248). Washington was not totally against one's choice to receive a liberal arts education in the sciences, math, and other fields of study, but he did not see their usefulness and practicality at that time (Franklin and Moss 246, 248). Because of these views, Washington faced criticism from other powerful African-American leaders, the most noteworthy being W.E.B. DuBois.

While DuBois credited Washington with gaining many followers and becoming successful, he disapproved of Washington's program for success. DuBois said Washington's philosophy contributed to the fallacy of African-American inferiority, "becoming a gospel of Work and Money [sic.] to such an extent as apparently almost completely to overshadow the higher aims of life" (DuBois 87). DuBois said Washington wanted blacks to give up their fight for political power, civil rights, and higher education opportunities for black youth in exchange for an industrial education and economic stability (DuBois 87). What purpose would economic empowerment serve if blacks did not possess political, civil, and educational rights? For these reasons, DuBois' philosophy revolved around cultivating the mind through liberal arts instruction. A graduate of Fisk University, a private black liberal arts institution in Nashville, Tennessee, DuBois learned the value of the classics and history. Being knowledgeable about and receiving degrees in these subject matters would contribute to the prosperity of blacks. DuBois dubbed this "The Talented Tenth," which Quarles describes as those college-bred men and women "who would furnish the leaven for the rise of the race" (173). Stating that "no secure civilization can be built in the South with the Negro as an ignorant, turbulent proletariat," DuBois urged Washington to realize that none of the black schools, including Tuskegee, which focused on industrial training, could exist without the liberal arts education of black teachers (DuBois 88-89, 135). Neither accepting nor rejecting Washington's way of thinking, DuBois said that blacks should support Washington in his preaching of "Thrift, Patience, and Industrial Training [sic.] for the masses." Yet, within the same breath, DuBois declared that Washington must be opposed as long as he justified America's injustices and resisted the cultivation of black minds (DuBois 94). These injustices were deeply ingrained in the educational system, as seen in the unequal status of the schools. The following excerpt of Dudley Randall's poem, "Booker T. and W.E.B." illustrates a more brief and concise description of these two viewpoints:

"It seems to me," said Booker T.,
"It shows a mighty lot of cheek
To study chemistry and Greek

When Mister Charlie needs a hand
To hoe the cotton on his land,
And when Miss Ann looks for a cook,
Why stick your nose inside a book?"

"I don't agree," said W.E.B.,
"If I should have the drive to seek
Knowledge of chemistry or Greek,
I'll do it. Charles and Miss can look
Another place for hand or cook.
Some men rejoice in skill of hand,
And some in cultivating land,
But there are others who maintain
The right to cultivate the brain."
(Randall 470)

During this country's "Separate, But Equal" Era, the educational system was not immune to the effects of segregation. Public black institutions had to cope with disparate funding, resources, and facilities: "Black public colleges also received unequal funding from state treasuries, through federal land-grant provisions, and from other federal sources. Many public HBCUs remained controlled by whites who believed in black inferiority" (Roebuck and Murty 29). With the 1954 Supreme Court ruling in *Brown v. Board of Education*, all public schools were ordered to desegregate because the high court ruled that "separate, but equal" was unconstitutional. Thus, the doors of many predominantly white colleges and universities were opened for African Americans. With desegregation, the prevailing thought was that all American institutions, and especially schools, would no longer be racially identifiable.

References

Books

Davis, Robert Bob. "Social Support Networks and Undergraduate Student Academic-Success-Related Outcomes: A Comparison of Black Students on Black and White Campuses." *College in Black and White: African American Students in Predominantly White and in Historically Black Public Universities*. Eds. Walter R. Allen, Edgar G. Epps, and Nesha Z. Haniff. Albany, NY: State University of New York Press, 1991. 143-157.

DuBois, W.E.B. *The Souls of Black Folk*. 1903. New York: Nal Penguin Inc., 1969.

Franklin, John Hope, and Alfred A. Moss, Jr. *From Slavery to Freedom: A History of Negro Americans*. 6th ed. New York: McGraw-Hill Inc., 1988.

Garibaldi, Antoine. "Black Colleges: An Overview." *Black Colleges and Universities: Challenges for the Future*. Ed. Antoine Garibaldi. New York: Praeger Publishers, 1984. 3-9.

Kannerstein, Gregory. "Black Colleges: Self-Concept." *Black Colleges in America: Challenge, Development, Survival*. Eds. Charles V. Willie and Ronald R. Edmonds. New York: Teachers College Press, 1978. 29-50.

Quarles, Benjamin. *The Negro in the Making of America*. 3rd ed. New York: Macmillan Publishing Company, 1987.

Randall, Dudley. "Booker T. and W.E.B." *Black Voices: An Anthology of Afro-American Literature*. Ed. Abraham Chapman. New York: Nal Penguin Inc., 1968. 470-471.

Roebuck, Julian B., and Komanduri S. Murty. *Historically Black Colleges and Universities: Their Place in American Higher Education*. Westport, CT: Praeger Publishers, 1993.

Walther, Erskine S. *Some Readings on Historically Black Colleges and Universities*. Rev. ed. Greensboro: Management Information and Research, June 1994.

Legal Cases and Statutes

Land Grant Act of 1862. United States Statutes at Large. Thirty-seventh Congress, Chapter 130. 503-505. 1862.

Land Grant Act of 1890. United States Statutes at Large. Fifty-first Congress, Chapter 841. 417-419. 1890.

HBCU Graduates and Enrollment

The enrollment patterns of African Americans attending college has changed drastically with more African Americans attending predominantly white schools than HBCUs. This is due largely in part to desegregation during the 1950s and 1960s. Even so, according to NAFEO's (National Association for Equal Opportunity in Higher Education), Research Department and Enrollment Information, 280,342 students enrolled in HBCUs in the fall of 1996. And, at the HBCU sister schools -- predominantly black institutions -- there were 88,195 enrollees, totaling 368,537 students. Three years earlier, there were 277,261 students attending historically black colleges. The approximate racial/ethnic distributions were as follows: 1.7 percent Hispanic, .16 percent Native American, 13 percent white, .78 percent Asian Pacific, 3 percent other, and 81 percent African American (Cunningham 29).

This ethnic representation at HBCUs has changed very little over the years. Granted, this may be a small percentage of all American college students. However, the success and strength of HBCUs is more accurately reflected in the number of baccalaureate degrees they confer to African Americans:

> While these institutions enroll only 20 percent of the nation's African-American undergraduates, they produce more than a third of its black college graduates. From 1986 to 1990, of the top 10 U.S. baccalaureate institutions that sent African-Americans [sic.] to graduate school and to receive doctorates, nine were HBIs [Historically Black Institutions]. (Wagener and Smith 42)

As can be expected at any institution with a significant number of students belonging to a particular ethnicity/race, a higher percentage of the majority population will receive the most degrees. This is true for HBCUs. However, what makes HBCUs unique is the percentage of students from other backgrounds who receive degrees as well. For example, in 1989, the 109 historically black colleges and universities awarded a total of 23,246 degrees, of which 3,797 (16 percent) were given to whites (Roebuck and Murty 97).

Before colleges and universities were integrated in the 1960s, historically black institutions were responsible for creating the African-American middle class in this country ("Desegregating Black" 26). Indeed, HBCUs are continuing to carry on this legacy, which is evident not just in the amount of HBCU graduates who go on to receive post-baccalaureate degrees but also in those who enter the business and professional arenas. Black colleges and universities are responsible for educating many African-American undergraduates and graduate students. For example, HBCU graduates compose: 75 percent of all African-American Ph.D's, 50 percent of African-American engineers, 50 percent of the nation's African-American business executives, 45 percent of African-American Congressional members, 50 percent of African-American elected officials, 80 percent of African-American federal judges, 75 percent of African-American lawyers, 85 percent of African-American physicians; and 75 percent of African-American military officers ("The Historically Black Colleges and Universities: A Future" 51; United States Air Force 2). *For a more comprehensive, but not exhaustive listing of notable alumni of historically black colleges and universities, see Appendix B.*

Even with this progression, there is also regression, as seen in the *U.S. v. Fordice* case. Many contend that HBCU administrators and supporters adhere to a separatist philosophy -- not willing to accept the changes taking place in this diverse, multicultural society. According to William Goodman, the lead attorney for Mississippi's Board of Trustees of State Institutions, also known as the State Board:

> If Black [sic.] students of yesterday received an inadequate education, it was the fault of white people. But today, if an inadequate education is what awaits Black [sic.] students, it will be the fault of certain Blacks [sic.] in power who push for quantity instead of quality. (Hawkins, "The Trial" 13-14)

Despite these differing opinions, many HBCUs are experiencing an increase in white students, and contrary to popular belief, HBCUs have always advocated diversity and inclusiveness. Perhaps Charles V. Willie, referring to black colleges and universities as "islands of integration in a sea of segregation," said it best: "They brought black and white teachers together and showed in their own way what can be accomplished when racial groups cooperate. The predominantly black public institutions of higher education have welcomed a considerable number of whites into their student bodies" (264). That is, HBCUs have never legally mandated, unlike other American institutions of higher learning, that one could not be admitted on the basis of race or ethnic background. In addition, Briggs and Robinson state there was a 60 percent increase, or 5.2 percent per year, of whites attending HBCUs from 1976 to 1990 (28). Moreover, according to the National Center for Education Statistics, in 1993, whites consisted of 13 percent of the HBCU enrollment, as compared to African-American students who made up only 8 percent of enrollment at majority institutions. Similarly, the same diversity patterns can be observed in the faculty at HBCUs. The President's Board of Advisors report that in 1993, the full-time faculty ratio was 91 percent white, non-Hispanic to 3.8 percent black, non-Hispanic at majority institutions in the southern border states. Conversely, in these same states, white, non-Hispanic faculty comprised approximately 40 percent of HBCU faculties (15, 16).

Also refuting the argument that black colleges and universities reject multiculturalism, Roebuck and Murty point out that in 1989, there were 11,041 full-time HBCU faculty members at all HBCUs, consisting of 61 percent African American, 29 percent white, and 10 percent other. These numbers were somewhat similar for the 2,961 part-time faculty -- 58 percent, 37 percent, and 5 percent, respectively (105, 107). It is important to note that these proportions are not only significant, but revealing as well, especially given the fact that HBCUs make up 3 percent of all American colleges and universities. Even with diversity, however, issues are bound to arise, especially when various groups of people are forced to relate and intermingle in a college/university setting.

Diversity Issues and Race Relations

Diversity is not a foreign or unheard of concept at HBCUs. Throughout black institutions' existence, there has always been an awareness of multiculturalism. After all, most of these postsecondary facilities were largely established by the Caucasian power structure -- federal government agencies, religious organizations -- and many had white presidents and administrators throughout the early part of the 20th century. However, this does not mean that these institutions are utopian. On the contrary, a closer look at the diverse culture found on most present-day campuses reveals much about racial attitudes, perceptions, and even more importantly, demonstrates how whites (the majority in mainstream America) adjust and cope with being the minority at black colleges.

Race Relations: Attitudes and Perceptions of Blacks and Whites at HBCUs

In observing the interrelationships between black and white faculty members and students at HBCUs, it is not shocking to find that forced integration can be a volatile and sensitive issue. Roebuck and Murty, in interviewing 400 faculty members and students on 15 southern campuses (five black private, five black public, and five white public) attempted to assess the state of race relations and the variety of viewpoints held by black and white faculty and students at HBCUs. Of all the groups affected by integration efforts, often times black students feel the most threatened. Roebuck and Murty found that 80 percent of the 150 black student respondents classified their white classmates as students but also "aliens" or "outsiders," 13 percent saw them as potential friends, and approximately 7 percent perceived them as "racial enemies" who didn't belong. As echoed in some of the interviews in this book, black students saw white students as competition for already limited scholarships (151, 152). Tables 3.1-3.4 provide a brief summary of Roebuck and Murty's most pertinent findings. (The "N.A.," or not applicable, indicates that no statistics were provided in these areas.)

Table 3.1:	Interracial/Intraracial Perceptions of Black and White Students at HBCUs	
Perceptions	**Blacks (n=150)**	**Whites (n=50)**
*White students ("aliens/outsiders")	80%	N.A.
*White faculty ("fair/competent")	90%	84%
*Black students ("minority in world/ dominant on campus")	N.A.	70%
*Black faculty ("fair/competent/ helpful")	N.A.	80%

Source: Roebuck and Murty 151, 153, 166, 167.

Table 3.2: Black Faculty's Interracial Perceptions of White Students at HBCUs	
Black Faculty's Perceptions (n=75)	**Percentage with Perceptions**
*"Different, but legitimate"	56%
*"Equal students"	26.6%
*"Questionable, but legitimate students"	10.6%
*"Aliens"	6.6%

Source: Roebuck and Murty 182-183.

Table 3.3: Black Faculty's Perceptions of White Faculty at HBCUs	
Black Faculty's Perceptions (n=75)	**Percentage with Perceptions**
*"Competent Professionals/Potential Friends"	81.3%
*"Worthy Colleagues Only"	14.6%
*"Aliens"	4%

Source: Roebuck and Murty 184.

Table 3.4: White Faculty's Perceptions of Black Faculty at HBCUs	
White Faculty's Perceptions (n=50)	**Percentage with Perceptions**
*"Dominant/Favored Group"	100%
*"Cultural Differences -- No Impact on Cooperation"	66%
*"Professional Colleagues/Potential Friends"	18%
*"Professional Colleagues Only"	16%
*"Blacks Favored in Recruitment, Hiring, Promotions, Leadership Roles"	62%
*"Black Faculty -- 'aloof and cold' in formal/informal settings"	14%

Source: Roebuck and Murty 193.

Race Relations: White Students' Experiences at HBCUs

For the most part, white students seem to experience a lesser amount of racial intolerance on black campuses than black students on predominantly white campuses. As a result, white students tend to have relatively positive academic and social experiences at black colleges. Libarkin's 1979 study of ten white students at Bowie State University, a public HBCU in Bowie, Maryland, affirms this. Examining academic perceptions, social experiences, and racial attitudes, Libarkin found that eight out of ten students felt their academic preparation was consistent with their expectations. Even more important, 90 percent felt they were more open-minded about and appreciative of diverse cultures. As for social interaction, eight did have contact with black and white students on campus and six did not perceive any racial attitudes or tension; black students "helped them adjust to campus life" (91). Similarly, Nixon and Henry polled administrators at nine HBCUs with white student populations of 15 to 35 percent to gauge overt racial incidents toward white students. Consistent with Libarkin's findings, none of the respondents reported overt racial incidents (distribution of discriminatory literature, verbal abuse, physical aggression) on campus that targeted whites (121, 122).

Classification and Adjustment of White Faculty at HBCUs

Not unlike the white students at black institutions, white faculty members seem to adjust fairly well. Even so, as university employees, they must contend with many daily issues that

16

white students are rarely exposed to. Smith and Borgstedt discussed some of the factors which contribute to the adjustment and satisfaction or dissatisfaction of these faculty members. Ninety-four white faculty members at six historically black colleges and universities responded to Smith and Borgstedt's questionnaire, which evaluated the faculty members' attitudes and perceptions about their personal lives (background information), professional lives, and current job. An overwhelming 75 percent reported feeling socially accepted and 92 percent were dedicated to and supportive of their university's goals and mission (156, 158). Nevertheless, some believed they would be more loyal to a predominantly white university and promotion or advancement opportunities were limited for them simply because they were white. Sixty percent of the white faculty described the administration as being "more rigid" and authoritarian than administrators at white institutions (158, 159).

Warnat discusses another detrimental facet of the black college climate that white faculty must battle. Often, white faculty members are classified according to their roles and others' perceptions of them. He categorizes them as the following:

- Moron -- The scapegoat; often considered to be too incompetent to obtain a position at a "better quality university" -- white university (335).
- Martyr -- Is burdened by racial guilt and accepts responsibilities and other tasks without complaining, for this is his/her moral obligation to the African-American community. Classified as the easiest for black faculty to accept and sympathize with (336).
- Messiah -- He/she feels that it is his/her duty to save and correct the heathens and uncivilized at black colleges. More specifically, messiahs "attempt to provide the direction which they feel has been lacking. . . . Their mission is perceived as 'bringing in the sheep'" (336). He/she is usually not well-received by their black colleagues.
- Marginal Man -- The middle-of-the-road faculty member, or a reflection of two cultures (the white social structure and a black college professor). He/she integrates the differing perspectives by not assimilating, but rather trying to understand the cultural environment he/she works in. By focusing on the similarities between the two cultures, he/she becomes the link (336, 337).

Diversity has always been a part of the HBCU atmosphere. However, its presence on campuses does not always alleviate racial tensions and feelings. In these environments, it is evident that the dominant culture is African American and the ultimate mission is to primarily serve these students. One black faculty member in Roebuck and Murty's study had this to say about black students: "We seek out our students on the campus and off the campus. We want them to know we love them, we care for them, and we are behind them in every way. . . . We take them as they are and try to improve them" (186). In addition, 59 percent of black faculty members stated that black students could learn better at HBCUs, their teaching abilities were more effective at HBCUs, and it was their duty to pass on and preserve their cultural heritage (181). These recurring themes of nurturance, acceptance, and culture may not be easily severed as integration efforts become more commonplace at the public black colleges. Yet, white faculty and other minority faculty members can not be disregarded either. Although most non-black faculty are often supportive of the HBCUs' educational mission and feel socially accepted, there are others who are disillusioned with the favoritism shown toward blacks. One commented:

There is no way to win on a black campus. If you try to be nice, they think you want something from them. If you act neutral about the race question, they accuse you of insensitivity. If you sympathize with them, you are patronizing. If you criticize them, you are a racist. (Roebuck and Murty 199)

The aforementioned diversity patterns and racial climate are representative of most black colleges and universities. While there may be imperfections and problems, it is evident that HBCUs are dedicated to embracing diversity -- to a certain extent. The task of incorporating diversity should not sacrifice the HBCU story and history. To many black college supporters, HBCUs have become too diverse, as more and more institutions are no longer historically black because of their racial compositions. For example, some of these schools include: West Virginia State College, Bluefield State College (West Virginia), Kentucky State University, Missouri's Lincoln University, and Oklahoma's Langston University. During the 1997-1998 academic year, Bluefield State and Lincoln University became focal points of discussion in the black higher education arena. Bluefield State's student population was approximately 92 percent Caucasian and 7 percent African American. While the administration was about 8 percent African American, there were no African-American faculty members. Lincoln University fared a little better. Nonetheless, out of almost 3,000 students, only 23 percent were African American. As a result of these percentages, administrators at these historically black institutions have found themselves in the awkward position of trying to find feasible methods to recruit more African American students and faculty. Black college supporters do not want to see this trend continue. However, other schools, like Tennessee State University in Nashville, may be well on their way to joining this list (Briggs and Robinson 28; Mercer, "The Ambiguous" A32; Schneider A12; Ahmad A1).

References

Books

Roebuck, Julian B., and Komanduri S. Murty. *Historically Black Colleges and Universities: Their Place in American Higher Education.* Westport, CT: Praeger Publishers, 1993.

Willie, Charles V. "Uniting Method and Purpose in Higher Education." *Black Colleges in America: Challenge, Development, Survival.* Eds. Charles V. Willie and Ronald R. Edmonds. New York: Teachers College Press, 1978. 263-270.

Periodicals

Ahmad, Ishmael Lateef. "L.U. Black Enrollment Dips Below 24 Percent." *The St. Louis American* 22 May 1997: A1, A11.

Briggs, Jimmie, and Lori S. Robinson. "Black Colleges Under Fire." *Emerge* Sept. 1993: 26-31.

Cunningham, Kitty. "Are Black Public Colleges Turning White?" *Black Enterprise* Aug. 1993: 29.

"Desegregating Black Public Colleges: What Will It Mean?" *Civil Rights Digest* 7.2 (Winter 1975): 26-35.

Hawkins, B. Denise. "The Trial: Round Two for *Fordice* Mississippi Higher Education Back in Court." *Black Issues In Higher Education* 2 June 1994: 12-16.

"The Historically Black Colleges and Universities: A Future in the Balance." *Academe* Jan.-Feb. 1995: 49-58.

Libarkin, Barbara. "A Study of the Satisfaction Levels of White Students at a Traditionally Black Public College." *Integrateducation* 22.1-3 (Winter 1984): 89-94.

Mercer, Joye. "The Ambiguous Success of Desegregation at Tennessee State U." *The Chronicle of Higher Education* 5 May 1993: A32-A33.

Nixon, Harold L., and Wilma J. Henry. "White Students at the Black University: Their Experiences Regarding Acts of Racial Intolerance." *Equity & Excellence* 25.2-4 (Winter 1992): 121-123.

Schneider, Alison. "Critics Charge Bluefield State With Eradicating Its Tradition as a Black College." *The Chronicle of Higher Education* 19 Dec. 1997: A12.

Smith, Susan L., and Kaye W. Borgstedt. "Factors Influencing Adjustment of White Faculty in Predominantly Black Colleges." *Journal of Negro Education* 54.2 (1985): 148-163.

Wagener, Ursula, and Edgar E. Smith. "Maintaining a Competitive Edge: Strategic Planning for Historically Black Institutions." *Change* Jan.-Feb. 1993: 40-49.

Warnat, Winifred I. "The Role of White Faculty on the Black College Campus." *Journal of Negro Education* 45.3 (Summer 1976): 334-338.

Miscellaneous

National Association for Equal Opportunity in Higher Education. Research Department and Enrollment Information. Telephone interview. 30 Oct. 1997.

The President's Board of Advisors on Historically Black Colleges and Universities. *A Century of Success: Historically Black Colleges and Universities, America's National Treasure.* 1995-1996 Annual Report. Washington: Sept. 1996.

United States Air Force. Office of the Under Secretary. *Historically Black Colleges and Universities.* Washington: GPO, Jan. 1994.

> Desegregation means that black people are in control of black institutions and white folks are in control of theirs, and you co-mingle. Some white folks go to black schools and vice-versa. As long as the process is open, everything will work out fine. But, integration means the liquidation of black institutions and we're submerged. We have no identity. (Alvin Chambliss, lead plaintiffs' attorney in *Fordice*, qtd. in Briggs and Robinson 27)

There has been a struggle for equal access and educational opportunities in the American educational system for over a century. Segregation, or the notion of separate, but unequal facilities and services, and inequities in funding have become characteristics of the system and have been contested on several occasions. Several landmark court cases have changed and continue to alter American education as we know it. Beginning with the introduction and acceptance of "separate, but equal," and moving to the desegregation era in which African Americans demanded equal educational opportunities, this chapter will come full circle to the recent cases focusing on the integration of public HBCUs and the dismantling of states' dual systems of higher education. Only those cases having an impact on the universities analyzed in this book will be discussed.

"Separate, But Equal"/Segregation Era

Plessy v. Ferguson, 163 U.S. 537 (1896).

On June 7, 1892, a Louisiana man challenged the constitutionality of an 1890 Louisiana statute which stated that it was legal to have separate coaches on trains for white and black passengers. It also said that one was to ride only in those cars that were designated for a particular race. Anyone violating these rules could be subjected to fines or imprisonment. Plessy, a black, violated this statute when he sat in the white section. When asked by the conductor to move to the appropriate car, Plessy refused, was removed from the train with force, and imprisoned (538). On May 18, 1896, Supreme Court Justice Brown delivered a precedent-setting decision, which upheld "separate, but equal" as constitutional:

> We cannot say that a law which authorized or even requires the separation of the two races in public conveyances is unreasonable, or more obnoxious to the Fourteenth Amendment than acts of Congress requiring separate schools for colored children in the District of Columbia, the constitutionality of which does not seem to have been questioned, or the corresponding acts of state legislatures. (550-551)

Thus, this was the beginning of legalized segregation (*de jure*) in all public aspects of American life, including higher education.

Desegregation/Public HBCU Integration Era

Brown v. Board of Education, 347 U.S. 483 (1954).

   Brown v. Board of Education, decided on May 17, 1954, was the case which reviewed whether segregation in public schools hindered equal educational opportunities for black students. Although there were similar cases in South Carolina, Virginia, and Delaware, the lawsuit brought against the Topeka Board of Education (Kansas) resulted in the Supreme Court's intervention (486, 493).

   The plaintiffs, black elementary school children in Topeka, challenged a Kansas statute which provided for separate schools for blacks and whites in school districts with 15,000 or more people. In Topeka, the Board of Education opted for segregated public elementary schools and integrated secondary schools (486). The plaintiffs said that separate schools were not equal, could not be brought up to equal standards, and violated equal protection laws (488). Therefore, they wanted access to all public schools on a "nonsegregated basis" (487).

   Under the direction of Chief Justice Warren, who delivered the Court's opinion, the Supreme Court ruled that "in the field of public education the doctrine of 'separate, but equal' has no place. Separate educational facilities are inherently unequal" (495). Segregation did not provide equal educational opportunities for minority children, and it violated equal protection under the Fourteenth Amendment (483, 495). Taking this position, the Supreme Court overturned *Plessy v. Ferguson*.

Brown v. Board of Education, 349 U.S. 294 (1955).

   A year later (May 31, 1955), Chief Justice Warren reiterated the main points of the earlier decision and gave further instructions in regards to desegregating public school systems. In his decision, he stated that racial discrimination in public education was illegal and all local, federal, and state governments must change those laws which allowed this practice. Further, school districts were responsible for implementing plans that would eradicate discrimination. During this transition, courts were to monitor progress towards the established goals. Lastly, students were to be admitted to public schools "on a racially nondiscriminatory basis with all deliberate speed" (298, 299, 300-301).

Adams v. Richardson, 356 F. Supp. 92 (1973).

   It was not until 1970 that desegregation in higher education became a national issue. In this year, the NAACP Legal Defense Fund (now separate from the NAACP) filed a suit against Elliot L. Richardson, Secretary of the Department of Health, Education, and Welfare (HEW), charging that 10 states were still operating dual systems of higher education (Barnes 14). These states were Louisiana, Mississippi, Oklahoma, North Carolina, Florida, Arkansas, Pennsylvania, Georgia, Maryland, and Virginia. HEW required these states to submit desegregation plans within 120 days. Nonetheless, when this case was decided on February 16, 1973, five states -- Arkansas, Pennsylvania, Georgia, Maryland, and Virginia -- had submitted unacceptable plans. The remaining five states had not submitted any plans. Further, at the time of this ruling, HEW had not taken administrative action against these states and continued distributing federal funds to these 10 states, which violated Title VI of the Civil Rights Act of 1964. Title VI simply stated that the government was not to distribute federal funds to institutions which used discriminatory practices and that citizens were to be protected from discrimination by federally funded programs (*Adams* 94). Between the time of filing and rendering a ruling on this case, an *amicus curiae* brief was filed by members of NAFEO (National Association for Equal Opportunity in Higher Education), a consortium of all HBCUs. According to Preer, the brief opposed the Legal Defense Fund's assumptions:

> The brief challenged three of the Legal Defense Fund's basic premises:
> whether public school precedents provided suitable standards for higher education; whether black colleges could be implicated in systemwide discrimination; whether eliminating the racial identity of state colleges realistically promised to enhance educational opportunities for black youth. NAFEO argued that black colleges were not the perpetrators of segregation, but its victims, and could not be sacrificed in an effort to achieve integration. (202)

In 1977, the U.S. District Court for the District of Columbia informed HEW that because it had accepted inadequate and inefficient plans for some states, the criteria must be redefined. HEW did this and by 1980, the Department of Education (formerly HEW) had accepted six of the plans from the original states and added eight more states to the list, bringing the total to 18 states which had to submit plans to dismantle their segregated higher education systems. These states included: Texas, Missouri, South Carolina, Ohio, Kentucky, Delaware, West Virginia, and Alabama. It should be noted that none of the *Adams* states, as they are often called, lost federal funds because of violations to their states' desegregation plans (Barnes 15, 16). All of the aforementioned states have at least one public historically black institution. This case continued until its dismissal on December 11, 1987.

Adams v. Bennett, 675 F. Supp. 668 (1987).

In 1987, John H. Pratt, United States District Judge, closed this case after 17 years of litigation. Originally, the case dealt with HEW's refusal to discontinue Title VI fund distribution to institutions which discriminated on the basis of race. However, over the years, more plaintiffs intervened, claiming other civil rights injustices -- sexism and discriminatory practices based on disability status. In the end, there were 40 plaintiffs (individuals), eight plaintiff-intervenors, and five plaintiff-intervenor organizations (671). All of the plaintiffs accused William Bennett, Secretary of Education, with violating Title VI of the Civil Rights Act of 1964 by disbursing federal money to educational institutions which discriminated in the above-listed areas (675).

Judge Pratt agreed with the plaintiffs, stating that the Department of Education perpetuated unlawful practices "by providing financial assistance to educational institutions and states which engage in discriminatory practices. . . . [And] by failing to proceed against states which failed to comply with statewide plans for the institutions of higher education" (677). Even so, he said that cutting off these funds may not deter discriminatory policies and practices (677). At the same time, Pratt mentioned that past courts had expressed that desegregation should not be placed solely upon HBCUs and that states should look at the unequal status of HBCUs, realizing that "desegregation will diminish higher education opportunities for Blacks" (678). With this in mind, states must examine the importance of HBCUs, but also abide by the law. Building on this same premise, Pratt stated that black institutions had not been brought up to equal standards, making it more difficult for them to attract white students. The solution to this problem was in the hands of state legislatures, who could rectify the matter by upgrading HBCU facilities. Furthermore, poor physical plants and facilities were problems before the passage of the 1964 Civil Rights Act; therefore, the defendants could not be blamed for these inequities (678, 679).

Having stated these reasons, Pratt dismissed the case because there were no grounds for continuing the litigation. And, in 1990, an appeals court ruled that the federal government could not be sued for not punishing those states or universities in violation of Title VI (Barnes 15).

Adams v. Richardson -- **Kentucky State University**

On January 15, 1981, the Office of Civil Rights (the Department of Education) notified Kentucky's governor, stating that Kentucky continued to operate a dual system of higher education. In essence, the report called attention to predominantly black Kentucky State and the remaining predominantly white state institutions. As stated in the *Adams* ruling, Kentucky had to submit an acceptable desegregation plan. As a result, the Kentucky Council on Public Higher Education (CHE) focused on Kentucky State University as a solution to the problem. Initially, several options were suggested -- closure, merger, enhancement of Kentucky State's facilities and programs, and desegregation. From that point on, there were several important dates in Kentucky State's history. First, on February 24, 1981, a motion failed to close Kentucky State. Second, students protested peacefully on March 5, 1981 at the state Capitol to express their views about the proposed plans. Third, after rejecting seven proposals, Kentucky State University's administration and the CHE endorsed a plan on December 2, 1981 to enhance Kentucky State University. Last, on January 29, 1982, the plan was approved by the U.S. Department of Education. The plan suggested the following actions: Kentucky State would remain a small, liberal arts university, keep its graduate program in Public Administration, restructure its land-grant functions to complement its liberal arts emphasis, and reevaluate faculty, staff, and academic disciplines for efficiency (Hardin 70-71, 73, 74).

Adams v. Richardson -- **Central State University**

In 1994, nearly 14 years after the Department of Education's Office of Civil Rights included Ohio as an *Adams* state, the federal government looked into the disparities in facilities and funding at Central State University, one of 13 public institutions in the state and the only state HBCU (Funk 1A). In 1981, the Department of Education concluded that Ohio had been "maintaining Central State University as an institution for blacks and has dissuaded white students from choosing to attend the institution" (qtd. in Funk 12A). In addition, the Education Department called attention to the fact that Central State was overwhelmingly black (7.4 percent of the student body was white), while the other state universities were overwhelmingly white, averaging a student body that was 7.4 percent black. As in the other aforementioned cases, Ohio was ordered to desegregate Central State. Eventually, the case was referred to the Justice Department. Yet, pre-litigation was short-lived because other cases in the South took priority, namely *U.S. v. Fordice*, which many legal scholars say could set a precedent for other states with public HBCUs. According to Funk, Arthur Thomas, Central State's former president of ten years, said that the federal government had not officially notified him of a renewed interest in the matter (12A). Years later, legal and political intervention were necessary to expedite matters.

Over the years, Central State University's desegregation process had virtually gone unnoticed. In fact, one may venture to say it had been forgotten by the state and the federal government as well. However, in 1996, many of the university's historical problems resurfaced once more, thereby prompting the Education Department's Office of Civil Rights to reopen the case. Financial crises, deteriorating buildings and living conditions, and an enrollment decline made Ohio legislators question the university's existence. One such legislator, State Senator Gene Watts, vehemently suggested on several occasions either merging the university with nearby Wright State University or closure (Fisher and Miller, "Plan Irritates" 9A; Miller and Fisher, "School's Recovery" 22A).

The question at hand was "who is at fault?" Not surprisingly, the Office of Civil Rights blamed the state of Ohio, stating that Ohio largely contributed to the institution's problems by not providing the necessary financial backing **(including plans to eliminate debt, which was estimated at between $8-11 million at first)** and enhancing its academic programs. Once these issues were settled, Central State would be more successful at recruiting diverse students (Fisher and Miller, "Plan Irritates" 9A; Miller and Fisher, "Survival Plan" 5A). Furthermore, the Office of Civil Rights was disillusioned with Ohio because it had not submitted an acceptable desegregation plan to comply with Title VI of the Civil Rights Act of 1964. And, Raymond Pierce, Deputy Assistant Secretary for the Office of Civil Rights, expressed his dissatisfaction: "It is sad that Ohio and Mississippi would remain in company as the two states failing to address the mishappenings within their state's histories" (Fisher and Miller, "Plan Irritates" 1A).

On the contrary, state legislators argued that years of fiscal mismanagement and leadership by university presidents committing a multitude of faux pas, led to the institution's dilemma. In 1995, then-president Arthur E. Thomas, was literally forced to resign by Governor George Voinovich's administration due to the aforementioned issues. Reportedly, Thomas' administration improperly transferred funds from various accounts to pay utility and other basic operating expenses and failed to contribute to employee retirement funds. As a result, the university fell behind in payments, and was unable to meet its fiscal obligations, let alone restore campus buildings which had fallen into disrepair (Miller and Fisher, "School's Recovery" 22A).

Hoping to turn the situation around, Thomas' interim replacement, Herman Smith, was hired. Yet, he was unsuccessful in his attempts to remedy Central State's financial crises, and was fired 15 months later by the newly appointed Central State Board of Trustees in July 1996 (Governor Voinovich asked all old members to step down). From state officials' point of view, he too, had yielded to financial mismanagement. The state auditor and other representatives questioned his leasing of $200,000 of furnishings for the president's residence while dormitories closed for code violations before the fall 1996 quarter (Miller and Fisher, "School's Recovery" 22A; Fisher, "What Happened?" 19). After Smith's departure, Dr. George Ayers, a consultant, became the next and last interim president, staying in this position until a permanent replacement, John W. Garland, was hired in late August 1997 (Fisher, "Set Up" 10; Fisher "Central State Hires" 13).

Garland, a 1971 alumnus of Central State University, had many hurdles to overcome, namely the restrictions passed by the Ohio legislature in June of 1997. Table 4.1 provides a brief summary of what some of these regulations entailed:

Table 4.1: Ohio's Stringent Restrictions Imposed Upon Central State University

1. Raise admissions standards for all freshman classes entering in August 1998 and thereafter.

2. Meet the reduced attrition rate that is set by the Ohio Board of Regents and the university Board of Trustees.

3. Receive reaccreditation from the North Central Accrediting Agency during the 1997-1998 academic year.

4. Seek out methods and funding sources to restore its endowment fund to at least a level that is appropriate and comparable to institutions of similar size.

5. Develop an alumni campaign drive to raise funding/donations that are comparable to institutions of similar size.

6. Use allocated state money to eliminate its current debt (the state's Office of Management and Budget will oversee the university's finances).

7. Significantly reduce its student loan default rate from 28.5 percent to below 21 percent within the next four years.

8. Tailor all academic programs to three colleges only: Business, Education, and Arts and Sciences.

9. Reduce faculty to meet the new academic mission.

10. Forbidden to use any state funds for financial assistance for non-Ohio residents and off-campus housing/transportation costs.

11. Apply all student room-and-board fees towards maintenance of dormitories and cafeterias.

12. Reduce money spent on sports. This includes accepting no private or public funds for sponsorship of those sports -- football and baseball -- which have been "sanctioned" by the National Association of Intercollegiate Athletics, beginning July 1, 1997. Baseball and football will cease to exist for the time being.

Sources: Miller and Fisher, "Survival Plan" 5A; Fisher, "Set Up" 12.

Needless to say, many of Central State University supporters were deeply disturbed by this proposal. Perhaps the most upsetting element of the proposal was the harsh stipulation that **if the university failed to meet any of the restrictions, the Ohio Board of Regents could and would close Central State**. George Ayers, former interim president, deemed that these conditions "are putting a rope around the neck of the institution" (Fisher, "Set Up" 10). Coupled with possible closure, there were threats of state budget cuts for the college in upcoming years. In May 1997, university representatives, students, and alumni pleaded with state officials in Columbus to continue funding Central State University (Miller and Fisher, "School's Recovery" 22A).

Understanding the plight of Central State University, the Ohio General Assembly heard the pleas of university advocates and voted to allocate $28 million to Central State over the next two years. Six million of this money is earmarked for much-needed building repairs, especially for dormitories. Equally important, the closure language was amended, giving the institution 45 days to correct any stipulation-related problems before the Ohio Board of Regents initiated closure proceedings. Governor George Voinovich signed the budget as well. Since Voinovich was not completely pleased with all of the budget language, provisions for additional funding may be approved in next year's capital improvements bill (Healy, "Ohio Lawmakers" A32;

Miller, "Governor Signs" 1B).

Many external Central State supporters were pleased with these amendments, including the U.S. Department of Education's Office of Civil Rights. Raymond Pierce, the Deputy Assistant Secretary who has often discussed his dissatisfaction with the state, saying "the issue [at hand] is the harm that has been visited upon the students in the form of years of unequal treatment," viewed these latest changes as a positive step towards progress. Furthermore, these preservation efforts reduced the likelihood that the case would go to federal court (Fisher and Miller, "Plan Irritates" 9A; Fisher, "Federal Official" 1B). Agreeing, State Representative Tom Roberts (chair of the Ohio Black Caucus' CSU committee), stated: "A year ago, Central State was in financial ruin and for months we've been battling to keep it open. Tonight, we have a plan for recovery and, we believe, the resources to do it" (Miller, "Panel Eases" 1A).

Although Central State was granted a second chance at survival, the university and its administrators had many obstacles to overcome. Colleges and universities can not exist without a student body. During the fall quarter 1997, the institution faced a drastic drop in enrollment from 1,960 in the fall 1996 to a projected 1,100-1,200. The numbers for the freshman class were grimmer, as they decreased from 324 in 1996 to an estimated 200 or less.♦ The lower enrollment was largely due in part to students' uncertainty about Central State's continued existence, negative publicity, and the suspension of recruitment efforts during the crucial spring and summer months (Fisher, "CSU Struggles" 1B).

Furthermore, the Board of Trustees approved recommendations to terminate 19 non-tenured faculty and refused to endorse three years of faculty promotions and tenure. Personnel cuts could have an adverse effect on reaccreditation, which is scheduled for the 1997-1998 school year. Despite these issues, the new president, John Garland, believed in Central State's future and was optimistic that it would rise again to reclaim its former glory: "My first goal is to stabilize the university. . . . As an alumnus, I bring a commitment to the university that might not have been present in the last two or three years" (Fisher, "Garland Talks" 1B-2B).

In early 1998, Garland's vision for Central State began to take shape. There was restored confidence in the university, as demonstrated by support received from Central State alumni, the state of Ohio, and the federal government. Financially, the institution was in better shape than it had been. A balanced budget was adopted, alumni chapters raised more funds, and Ohio's Office of Budget and Management gave more fiscal control to university officials (Fisher, "Back from the Brink" 10; Fisher, "Central State Regains" 10).

On the legal front, the U.S. Department of Education's Office of Civil Rights opted to close its Title VI investigation at this time, while reserving its right to monitor the situation closely. This move seemingly eliminates the potential of a federal lawsuit. And, college administrators continue devising new strategies to assist in their recruitment efforts because the 1997 fall quarter enrollment was as projected (at approximately 1,052 students). These collaborative efforts will include alumni, a public relations committee, and a grant, which is one of the most unique survival formulas. The college has received a $1.5 million grant for an estimated 140 incoming freshman and community college transfer students with 3.0 GPAs to attend Central State for little or no expense during the next four years (Fisher, "Feds Close" 10; Fisher, "Back from the Brink" 10; WDTN/Channel 2 website). With renewed financial support from Ohio legislators for the next two years and a dedicated alumnus at the helm of the university, Central State University may be well on the road to recovery and survive into the 21st century.♦♦

***Geier v. Dunn*, 337 F. Supp. 573 (1972).**

> Depending on whom you talk to in this city, Tennessee State University is either a shining example of diversity or a sacrificial lamb. . . . Black-college supporters, here and elsewhere, are bothered by what they say is the narrow focus on making black colleges less black, while predominantly white colleges do not face the same pressure to become less white. That anxiety is crystallized here. (Mercer, "Ambiguous Success" A32)

The desegregation of higher education in Tennessee dates back to May 21, 1968. On this date, the plaintiffs, Tennessee State University professor Rita Sanders Geier and others, filed a suit against then-Tennessee governor Winfield Dunn and the chairman of the Trustee Board of the University of Tennessee. According to the plaintiffs, the construction of the University of Tennessee at Nashville not only would provide duplicate programs, but also would lead to the classification of UT Nashville and Tennessee State as identifiably white and black institutions, respectively. For these reasons, the plaintiffs sought an injunction to prevent the construction of UT Nashville (573). On July 22, 1968, the United States intervened as a plaintiff and asked the state to submit a desegregation plan.

The court did not prohibit the construction of UT Nashville, but required the state to submit a desegregation plan by April 1, 1969. The state was expected to place particular attention on then Tennessee A&I (State) University. As a result, the proposed plan stated that Tennessee State would "intensify its efforts" to recruit white students and faculty members, in addition to developing those programs which would attract area black and white students. And, the plan called for joint programs with Tennessee State, Austin Peay State University, UT Nashville, and Middle Tennessee State University that would ensure a racial balance. Once the plan was submitted, the court neither accepted nor rejected it, but told the state to rework it by April 1, 1970 (574-575). The new plan revealed that Tennessee State continued to remain predominantly black in the 1970-1971 school year, with 99.7 percent black students and 81 percent black faculty members. The white institutions remained predominantly white (576). These results prompted the court to intervene further. Also, it should be noted that although Tennessee faced some of the same issues as the other 18 *Adams* states, it was not included because its litigation predated the *Adams* lawsuit (Ivey 6).

On February 3, 1972, Judge Frank Gray, Jr. delivered a ruling, concluding that it was the responsibility of the state to dismantle its segregated higher education system, especially when such systems were rooted in the *de jure* (by law) segregation era. Yet, the state must also be mindful that the way to eliminate desegregation in higher education differs from those solutions applied to secondary educational systems. Thus, open door admissions policies, "good faith" recruiting strategies, and the inclusion of remedial programs in the curriculum were "sufficient as a basic requirement" in eradicating segregation. Nonetheless, if these requirements fail to achieve the established goals, other options must be implemented. For example, in regards to Tennessee State, Gray stated that the state's plans had not worked, probably would never work, and the current student body composition violated the constitution (579-580). Further, he said white students would not be attracted to a black institution unless there was a significant "white presence" on campus (581). For these reasons, Gray suggested a merger of UT Nashville and Tennessee State. This merger was finalized on July 1, 1979 (*TSU 1993-1995 Undergraduate Catalog* 4).

Litigation did not end with the merger of UT Nashville and Tennessee State University. In

1984, there was a Stipulation of Settlement which required the desegregation of all state universities and an annual review by a court-appointed committee (Mercer, "Contradictory Proposals" A24). Some Tennessee State faculty headed back to court in 1995, claiming that Tennessee State University faculty and administration were not in total compliance with the settlement, as seen in the insubstantial white undergraduate enrollment at Tennessee State University. The plaintiffs asked for a merger between Tennessee State University and Middle Tennessee State University. In addition, other requests included but were not limited to: a major recruitment campaign for Tennessee State in Davidson County (Nashville), more money to institute a registration and financial aid system comparable to those at Middle Tennessee State, and an elimination of duplicative programs ("Tennessee State University National Alumni Legal Update" 1-2). Many significant administrative officials opposed this merger, including Tennessee State University President James A. Hefner, state officials, and the lawyer of Rita Sanders Geier, the original plaintiff. In 1994, while approximately 10 percent of Middle Tennessee State's 17,500 students was black, about 32 percent of Tennessee State's 7,500 undergraduates were white (Mercer, "Contradictory Proposals" A24). *A more comprehensive breakdown of past graduates, faculty members, and enrollment at Tennessee's state institutions is provided in Appendix C.*

U.S. v. Fordice, 112 S. Ct. 2727 (1992).

On January 28, 1975, Jake Ayers, Sr. and 21 African-American Mississippi college students filed a lawsuit against the governor of Mississippi, charging that Mississippi continued to operate a racially segregated higher education system which violated the Fifth, Ninth, Thirteenth, and Fourteenth Amendments. In April of that same year, the United States intervened on the plaintiffs' side, stating that Mississippi had violated the Fourteenth Amendment and Title VI of the Civil Rights Act of 1964. For 12 years thereafter, all parties attempted to reach an out-of-court resolution (Hawkins, "The Trial" 14; *Fordice* 2733).

One such solution was the establishment of "Mission Statements" in 1981. The state classified the eight public universities into the following categories: comprehensive, urban, and regional. The University of Mississippi, Mississippi State University, and the University of Southern Mississippi were classified as comprehensive, or those institutions with the most extensive resources and programs. The lone urban university, Jackson State University (an HBCU), had limited research programs. As regional institutions, Delta State University, Mississippi University for Women, and historically black Alcorn State University and Mississippi Valley State University, served as undergraduate institutions with limited programs. Even though the state reasoned that this would help alleviate problems associated with a dual system, it did not. During the mid-1980s, 99 percent of Mississippi's white students were at the five historically white institutions (80 to 91 percent white student body), while 71 percent of Mississippi's black students attended the three HBCUs, which had student bodies that were 92 to 99 percent black (2733, 2734).

The *Ayers* case went to trial in a U.S. District Court (Oxford, Mississippi) on April 27, 1987. Judge Neal Biggers, Jr. presided. While the petitioners said the state still maintained racially discriminatory practices in its higher education system, the defendants said the state had fulfilled the objectives in its desegregation plan by implementing race-neutral admissions and hiring policies (2734). More than 70 witnesses testified in this five-week trial. On December 11, 1987, Biggers dismissed the case, ruling that the state had not violated any federal law and was successfully working toward dismantling its dual higher education system. The case did not end here, as a Court of Appeals further concluded that the state had done enough and that race-neutral policies, although not sufficient for desegregating secondary school systems, were adequate for higher education institutions. That is, the same standards could not be applied to different levels of educational institutions. After this decision, the case was appealed and argued before the U.S. Supreme Court on November 13, 1991 (Hawkins, "The Trial" 14; *Fordice* 2735, 2736).

Writing the majority opinion (8 to 1), Justice Byron White ruled (on June 26, 1992) that the adoption and implementation of race-neutral admissions and hiring policies were not enough to eliminate a segregated system (2736). And, the Court ruled that while these practices sounded good on paper, in actuality Mississippi's policies still fostered segregation:

> There are several surviving aspects of Mississippi's prior dual system which are constitutionally suspect; for even though such policies may be race-neutral on their face, they substantially restrict a person's choice of which institution to enter and they contribute to the racial identifiability of the eight public universities. Mississippi must justify these policies or eliminate them. (2738)

The Court called attention to the state's admissions policies, consistency of the mission statements, program duplication, and whether eight public universities were needed (2738).

At the time the Court made its decision, Mississippi universities relied only on ACT scores in determining admission to a particular university. For the most part, high school grade point averages were not taken into account. The minimum ACT standards were enacted in 1963, before Title VI of the 1964 Civil Rights Act. A student could attend the three comprehensive universities and Delta State only if he or she received at least a 15 on the ACT. Mississippi University for Women required a grade point average of 3.0 or an ACT score of 18. And, for admission to the three HBCUs, a student must have scored at least a 13 for automatic admission --although students with lower scores could still be admitted. According to the Court, these standards were extremely unfair, especially since in 1985, 72 percent of white students scored a 15 or higher, while approximately 70 percent of black students scored lower than that score (2739, 2740). This meant that most black students had no choice but to attend the HBCUs. Table 4.2 shows the average score for black and white Mississippians in 1963, when the standards were established, and in 1992, when the Court rendered a decision.

Table 4.2:	Average ACT Scores for Black and White Mississippi Students in 1963 and 1992	
	Blacks	**Whites**
1963	7	18
1992	16.3	20

Sources: *Fordice* 2738; Boulard and Hawkins 9.

Closely aligned with the ACT scores were the mission statements, which White pointed out were not consistent. For example, the regional universities -- Alcorn, Mississippi Valley, Delta State, and Mississippi University for Women (MUW) -- had different minimum ACT scores. MUW required an 18, Delta State a 15, and the two HBCUs a 13 (2739). From the Court's stance, these scores and the others as well needed to be justified "in terms of sound educational policy" (2740). Also, the Court noted that different mission statements would limit students' choice of universities (2742).

Program duplication was another issue the Court examined. White found that many undergraduate and graduate programs were "unnecessarily duplicated," and were probably a result of the "separate, but equal" philosophy. To support his view, White cited the District Court's findings that 34.6 percent of black institutions' undergraduate programs as well as 90 percent of black institutions' graduate programs were duplicated at the white universities (2740-2741).

Last, White said that Mississippi needed to reassess the need for eight public institutions. After all, some of these universities, like Delta State and Mississippi Valley; and Mississippi State and Mississippi University for Women, are in close proximity to one another. Hence, a remedy could be closure or merger (2742, 2743).

The Court did not provide a definitive ruling. However, White did say that it was the state's responsibility to dismantle dual educational systems:

> That an institution is predominantly white or black does not in itself make out a constitutional violation. But surely the State [sic.] may not leave in place policies rooted in its prior officially-segregated [sic.] system that serve to maintain the racial identifiability of its universities if those policies can practicably be eliminated without eroding sound educational policies. (2743)

Having said this, White sent the case back to the District Court to reexamine those aspects which were constitutionally questionable.

On May 9, 1994, Biggers once again heard testimony regarding *U.S. v. Fordice* (Hawkins, "The Trial" 14). Before rendering his decision, Biggers observed some of the differences among Mississippi's state-supported black and white universities. In December 1994, he visited six of the eight campuses (Boulard and Hawkins 6). During the course of the case, both the State College Board and the plaintiffs submitted proposals for change. The College Board proposed to close Mississippi Valley and merge it with Delta State; whereas, the plaintiffs wanted to keep all of the universities open and enhance the programs and curriculum at the three HBCUs (Hawkins, "A Quest" 12-13). ***See Appendix D for a more detailed outline of the original plans.*** Needless to say, many HBCU advocates were deeply upset by the possible closure of Mississippi Valley, for Vice President Dr. Roy C. Hudson said: "Here in the Mississippi Delta -- the most depressed area in the country, with the lowest educational achievement and legacy of plantations -- this institution helps people overcome. You can't close this institution. It's morally, educationally and economically unsound" (Hawkins, "Turning Point" 13).

Likewise, the plaintiffs' lead attorney, Alvin O. Chambliss, Jr., was upset by some developments, namely the early implementation of tougher admissions standards -- a 16 on the ACT or a 3.2 grade point average. Chambliss said that the new policies could decrease the amount of black students admitted to universities by half and that additional high school graduation requirements would be detrimental, as predominantly black school districts lack certain courses in their curriculum. Biggers heeded these concerns and on December 13, 1994, ruled that the College Board must halt the new admissions standards for the time being (Boulard and Hawkins 7, 8).

After months of awaiting the U.S. District Court ruling, black college supporters in Mississippi and throughout the country received good news about the fate of the three black public institutions in Mississippi. On March 7, 1995, Biggers ruled that all eight state institutions would remain open and operate as separate entities. By doing so, Biggers rejected the proposal to merge Mississippi Valley and Delta State, and Mississippi University for Women and Mississippi State University. According to Biggers, mergers would neither alleviate segregation nor promote integration (Jaschik, "Ruling in Mississippi" A23).

In addition, his 187-page decision called for several actions. First, Biggers required the state legislature to provide more financial backing for Alcorn State and Jackson State. Second, in keeping with more funding, Biggers suggested additional programs at Jackson State, namely doctoral programs in social work, urban planning and business, as well as programs in law, pharmacy, and engineering. Biggers contended that these programs could be used as initiatives to attract more white students to Jackson State. On the contrary, he rejected the idea of transferring the University of Mississippi's medical school to Jackson State. Third, Biggers endorsed the new admissions standards, which he halted in early December 1994. These criteria use a certain GPA and ACT scores in determining a student's admission to the state universities. Further, those who do not meet these prerequisites have the option of successfully completing summer remedial classes to correct their academic deficiencies (Jaschik, "Ruling in Mississippi" A23, A24).

Fourth, although Mississippi Valley was spared from closure and a merger, it did not fare as well as the other two HBCUs, receiving no extra funding. Moreover, Biggers' major suggestion for the university was to provide more minority scholarships to attract white students. The State Board (Board of Trustees of State Institutions of Higher Learning) offered little more hope for Mississippi Valley, as officials proposed a study to determine the most optimistic future for the university. Last, Biggers ordered the development of a desegregation monitoring committee to report the state institutions' desegregation progress. Further, he said that if other options regarding Mississippi Valley fail, a merger between Mississippi Valley and Delta State could be feasible; however, this alternative and others must be brought before the desegregation monitoring committee and his court (Jaschik, "Ruling in Mississippi" A23, A24).

Although the fate of Mississippi's public HBCUs is unknown, there are aspects of the *Fordice* case which remain unquestionable. First, many HBCU supporters say that the push for diversity is not the problem, but rather economics -- money is needed to improve HBCU facilities, thereby attracting more diverse students (Boulard and Hawkins 9). Second, and perhaps even more important, advocates on both sides of this 24-year old case are growing weary and looking for common ground on which to settle these issues once and for all. U.S. Representative Bennie Thompson (MS), one of the plaintiffs, has said "I think it is time for all parties to sit down and see if we can put this case to rest" (Roach and Fields 10). Concurring with this stance, Marlin Ivey, president of the College Board (Mississippi Board of Trustees of State Institutions of Higher Learning), has stated "We want it [*Ayers*] over with" (Roach and Fields 10).

The Fifth U.S. Circuit Court of Appeals' latest decision, rendered on April 23, 1997, prompted these statements and feelings. Indeed, compromise may be the only solution. This decision was in response to the plaintiffs' appeal regarding uniform admissions standards -- 16 minimum ACT score and summer remedial programs (Roach and Fields 12; "Appeal" 18-19). That is, the decision reexamined Judge Biggers' March 1995 District Court ruling.

In short, the most important facets of Biggers' decision analyzed by the Appeals Court included admissions standards, remedial courses, scholarships, and enhancement of HBCUs. The three-judge panel concluded that consistent admissions policies, such as an ACT minimum score of 16 for all state universities, is acceptable and "educationally sound" as long as other alternative methods are utilized to ensure admission for those who do not score a 16. These methods may encompass grade point averages and the summer remediation courses, already implemented in Mississippi. Although this was not the outcome the plaintiffs hoped for, the judges did provide some consolation. If the remedial programs fail, the District Court must develop a new plan ("What the Court" 13; "Appeal" 19).

Closely aligned to the summer remedial programs is the existing academic year remedial courses. The District Court's ruling and also the College Board's proposal, implied that summer remediation would replace year-round remediation ("What the Court" 13; "Appeal" 20). Herein exists a problem, as the Fifth Circuit Appeals Court stated that the elimination of year-round remediation may result in discriminatory practices:

> Remedial courses may be an important part of the admissions policy at any school in which a significant number of students are not predicted to achieve a C average during their first year. . . . On remand, the district court [sic.] should determine if remedial courses are needed to help ensure that students admitted under the new admissions criteria have a realistic chance of achieving academic success. ("Appeal" 20)

Another point of contention has been the use of "ACT cutoff scores" as the sole determinant in scholarship awards. The predominantly white institutions in Mississippi used this standard in deciding one's eligibility. Consequently, because Mississippi Caucasian students have historically scored higher than their African-American counterparts, more Caucasian students are recipients of these scholarships. At the five white public institutions, minimum ACT requirements ranged from 18 to 31. Further, these incongruities became all the more evident when comparing the percentage of those first-time freshman who were African American versus the percentage of scholarship recipients for this same group. For example, in 1992-1993, the freshman class at University of Southern Mississippi was 27 percent African American; however, only 1 percent of scholarship recipients was African American. Thus, the judges reasoned that this practice may foster segregation and should be rectified by the 1998-1999 academic school year ("Appeal" 20-22; "What the Court" 13).

As for enhancing historically black institutions, the Fifth Circuit Court of Appeals judges acknowledged disparities in funding at the historically white institutions (HWIs) and HBCUs, but failed to suggest any remedies. From their stance, these funding differences were appropriate for the HBCUs because of their limited missions and lower enrollment. However, they suggested that the District Court find a solution for the inadequacies in facilities (libraries, equipment) at HBCUs. Moreover, once again the Appeals Court noted program duplication, stating that it too, was a remnant of *de jure* (by law) segregation. The District Court has been ordered to ensure the addition of new programs at Mississippi Valley and Alcorn State (Roach and Fields 14; "Appeal" 25; "What the Court" 13).

In essence, the Appeals Court concluded that Mississippi, albeit on the right path in some aspects, still needs to resolve some issues before its higher education system can be declared desegregated. Many plaintiffs agree with this, but are a bit doubtful if the dual system of higher education will ever be eradicated. Critics, such as Howard University Law professor Ken Tollett, say that the case emphasizes desegregating HBCUs, thereby making them more attractive to Caucasian students, but does not do likewise to historically white institutions: "This decision gives no consideration to the enhancement of schools for Blacks [sic.]. It all has to do with attracting more whites to Black [sic.] schools. I haven't seen anything about how to bring more

Black students in to white schools. . ." (Roach and Fields 14).

Despite these feelings of frustration, proponents on both sides are ready to move on. Growing tired of this case and ready for closure, the College Board refused to appeal the Fifth Circuit Court of Appeals ruling. The plaintiffs submitted petitions again, but the Appeals Court refused to reconsider any parts of its April 1997 ruling. Now, the plaintiffs -- both private and the Justice Department must decide if it is worth appealing to the Supreme Court again ("Mississippi Declines" 6; Healy and Strosnider A35). Perhaps the end of *Fordice* is nearing. For a condensed version of the important dates cited in this 24-year-old case, see Table 4.3.

Table 4.3: Important Dates in the *Fordice* Case	
*January 28, 1975	*Jake Ayers, Sr. and others file suit.*
*April 1975	*U.S. intervenes on plaintiffs' side.*
*August 26, 1986	*Jake Ayers, Sr. dies from a heart attack.*
*April 27, 1987	*Trial in District Court, Oxford, Mississippi.*
*December 11, 1987	*Case dismissed.*
*December 16, 1987	*Plaintiffs appeal in 5th U.S. Circuit Court of Appeals.*
*December 17, 1990	*Alvin O. Chambliss, Jr. (plaintiffs' attorney) appeals to U.S. Supreme Court.*
*November 13, 1991	*Arguments begin in Supreme Court.*
*June 26, 1992	*Supreme Court sends case back to District Court.*
*October 22, 1992	*College Board submits initial proposal.*
*April 7, 1994	*College Board submits revised proposal, and plaintiffs submit proposal as well.*
*May 9, 1994	*Trial begins in District Court.*
*December 1994	*Judge Biggers visits campuses.*
*March 7, 1995	*Judge Biggers rules all 8 state universities will stay open.*
*December 15, 1995	*Summer remedial plan is appealed by plaintiffs and the U.S. Department of Education.*
*February 1 and 16, 1996	*Fifth Circuit District Court denies appeal and plaintiffs later refile their appeal in the Fifth Circuit Court of Appeals.*
*September 4, 1996	*Judge Biggers asks for summer remedial programs "status reports." That of the plaintiffs reveals that the percentage of blacks eligible for enrollment under the new admissions standards has dropped 32 percent. The number of freshman enrollees also dropped in the fall 1996 both at the HBCUs and historically white institutions -- 14 and 9 percent, respectively.*
*November 22, 1996	*The College Board and an independent committee recommend that Jackson State University receive an engineering school, but not programs in law, pharmacy, and allied health.*

*April 23, 1997	*The U.S. Court of Appeals refuses to outlaw the admissions policies of the eight public universities, and concludes that the state should review enhancing programs at MVSU and develop new land grant programs at ASU.*
*May 1997	*Mississippi's College Board declines another appeal of the Fifth Circuit Court of Appeals most recent ruling.*
*September 1997	*Faction of plaintiffs planning to file petition with U.S. Supreme Court, asking them to review the case again.*
*January 1998	*U.S. Supreme Court declines review of the case.*

Sources: Hawkins, "The Trial" 14; Jaschik, "Ruling in Mississippi" A23; "Appeal" 18-19; "Mississippi Declines" 6; Healy, "Court Asked" A37; Lederman A28.

At Press Time:

♦The enrollment continues to experience ups and downs at Central State. The fall 1998 total student headcount was approximately 1,000, down slightly from the fall quarter of 1997. Nevertheless, the freshmen class was projected to nearly double that of the freshmen class of 1997. Estimates show that there were nearly 200 freshmen in the class of 2002, compared to less than 90 freshmen in the class of 2001 (Fisher, "Efforts Pay" 6A).

♦♦Central State is proving to the HBCU community and all academia that it is, indeed, a "phoenix rising." Since August 1997, President John Garland and his dedicated team have demonstrated that the university is a shining example of steadfastness and resilience. They have managed to accomplish many tasks that were no small feats. In fact, several of these achievements were seemingly impossible a little over a year ago. First and perhaps most importantly, the university has been reaccredited by the North Central Association of Colleges and Schools through 2003. It should be noted that without this provision, the state could have moved to close the university. Additionally, the university's manufacturing engineering program, the only one at an HBCU, was also reaccredited. Financially, Central State is stabilizing as well. With the permission of the U.S. Department of Education, the university can now receive faster and easier access to federal student financial aid programs, a lifesaver for students who are in dire financial need. And, as of the end of fiscal year 1998, which ended in June 1998, Central State managed a balanced budget, according to President Garland (Fisher, "Efforts Pay" 1A, 6A). This, too, was unheard of just a couple of years ago.

References

Books

Hardin, John A. *Onward and Upward: A Centennial History of Kentucky State University 1886-1986.* Frankfort: Kentucky State University, 1987.

Preer, Jean L. *Lawyers v. Educators: Black Colleges and Desegregation in Public Higher Education.* Westport, CT: Greenwood Press, 1982.

Periodicals

"Appeal from the United States District Court for the Northern District of Mississippi." *Black Issues In Higher Education* 15 May 1997: 15-25.

Barnes, Esmeralda. "Higher Education Gains for African Americans Erode Following Dismissal of *Adams,* Observers Say." *Black Issues In Higher Education* 8 Apr. 1993: 14+.

Boulard, Garry, and B. Denise Hawkins. "*Fordice* Judge Visits Black Campuses in Mississippi." *Black Issues In Higher Education* 29 Dec. 1994: 6-9.

Briggs, Jimmie, and Lori S. Robinson. "Black Colleges Under Fire." *Emerge* Sept. 1993: 26-31.

Fisher, Mark. "Back from the Brink: Having Survived a Life-Threatening '97, Central State Is Showing New Signs of Vitality." *Black Issues In Higher Education* 5 Feb. 1998: 10-11.

_____. "CSU Struggles for Enrollment." *Dayton Daily News* 18 Aug. 1997: 1B.

_____. "Central State Hires New President, Fires One-sixth of Faculty." *Black Issues In Higher Education* 21 Aug. 1997: 13.

_____. "Central State Regains Financial Control." *Black Issues In Higher Education* 19 Mar. 1998: 10.

_____. "Central State University: What Happened?" *Black Issues In Higher Education* 26 Dec. 1996: 17-19.

_____. "Efforts Pay Off at CSU." *Dayton Daily News* 8 Aug. 1998: 1A, 6A.

_____. "Federal Official Likes CSU Plan." *Dayton Daily News* 2 July 1997: 1B.

_____. "Feds Close Title VI Investigation in Ohio." *Black Issues In Higher Education* 19 Mar. 1998: 10-11.

_____. "Garland Talks Future at CSU." *Dayton Daily News* 19 Aug. 1997: 1B-2B.

_____. "Set Up to Fail? New Restrictions on Central State University Considered 'Punitive' by Supporters." *Black Issues In Higher Education* 26 June 1997: 10-13.

Fisher, Mark, and Tim Miller. "Plan Irritates Feds." *Dayton Daily News* 29 May 1997: 1A, 9A.

Funk, John. "U.S. Investigates Ohio's Treatment of Central State U." *The Plain Dealer* 25 Mar. 1994: 1A, 12A.

Hawkins, B. Denise. "A Quest for Equality." *Black Issues In Higher Education* 5 May 1994: 10-13.

_____. "The Trial: Round Two for *Fordice* Mississippi Higher Education Back in Court." *Black Issues In Higher Education* 2 June 1994: 12-16.

_____. "Turning Point: A High Court 'Victory' for Mississippi Sours." *Black Issues In Higher Education* 8 Apr. 1993: 12+.

Healy, Patrick. "Court Asked to Review Mississippi Desegregation Case." *The Chronicle of Higher Education* 26 Sept. 1997: A37.

_____. "Ohio Lawmakers Vote to Keep Central State U. Alive, but Demand Improvements." *The Chronicle of Higher Education* 3 July 1997: A32.

Healy, Patrick, and Kim Strosnider. "Court Declines Appeal in Desegregation Case." *The Chronicle of Higher Education* 27 June 1997: A35.

Ivey, Saundra. "Federal Court Upholds Order to Merge Black, White Campuses in Nashville." *The Chronicle of Higher Education* 30 Apr. 1979: 1, 6.

Jaschik, Scott. "Ruling in Mississippi." *The Chronicle of Higher Education* 17 Mar. 1995: A23-A25.

Lederman, Douglas. "High Court Bars Review of Mississippi Case." *The Chronicle of Higher Education* 30 Jan. 1998: A28.

Mercer, Joye. "The Ambiguous Success of Desegregation at Tennessee State U." *The Chronicle of Higher Education* 5 May 1993: A32-A33.

_____. "Contradictory Proposals Offered in Tennessee's College-Desegregation Case." *The Chronicle of Higher Education* 25 May 1994: A24.

Miller, Tim. "Governor Signs State Budget." *Dayton Daily News* 1 July 1997: 1B.

_____. "Panel Eases Terms for CSU." *Dayton Daily News* 20 June 1997: 1A, 10A.

Miller, Tim, and Mark Fisher. "School's Recovery Began on Act of Trust." *Dayton Daily News*

29 June 1997: 1A, 22A.

_____. "Survival Plan for School Pleases Both Sides." *Dayton Daily News* 28 May 1997: 1A, 5A.

"Mississippi Declines to Appeal *Fordice* Decision." *Black Issues In Higher Education* 29 May 1997: 6.

Roach, Ronald, and Cheryl D. Fields, et al. "Mississippi Churning." *Black Issues In Higher Education* 15 May 1997: 10-14.

"What the Court Decided in the *Fordice* Case." *Black Issues In Higher Education* 15 May 1997: 13.

Legal Cases and Statutes

Adams v. Bennett. 675 F. Supp. 668 (D.C. District Court, 1987).

Adams v. Richardson. 356 F. Supp. 92 (D.C. District Court, 1973).

Brown v. Board of Education. 347 U.S. 483 (1954).

Brown v. Board of Education. 349 U.S. 294 (1955).

Geier v. Dunn. 337 F. Supp. 573 (Middle District of Tennessee, Nashville Division, District Court, 1972).

Plessy v. Ferguson. 163 U.S. 537 (1896).

U.S. v. Fordice. 112 S. Ct. 2727 (1992).

Miscellaneous

"CSU Grant." *2News Total News Coverage*. Internet WWW page at: <http://wdtn.com/2news/newstoday.html> or <http://wdtn.com/wdtn/> (29 Apr. 1998).

Tennessee State University National Alumni Association Legal Update. Letter. Jan. 1995.

Tennessee State University 1993-1995 Undergraduate Catalog. Nashville: Tennessee State University.

Figuratively, black colleges have received only the crumbs from the tables of this nation's educational funds. . . . There has been no time in their histories when they did not need to be imperatively concerned about their survival. (Thompson 183)

I ndeed, this has been a common cry of many HBCU advocates -- inequity in not only funding but also in facilities, equipment, and resources that are desperately needed to compete with other institutions, namely predominantly white institutions. Yes, the Land Grant Act of 1890 and other federal provisions were established to ensure an equal distribution of federal funds among all public colleges and universities. Yet, many argue that the financial status of HBCUs is of little importance to federal and state governments. For example, Louis E. Armstrong, a graduate of Jackson State University and director of the Mississippi Legal Services Coalition, states that it is a matter of educational disparity: "This case [*U.S. v. Fordice*] points to obvious discrimination; just look at the laboratories, athletic fields and dormitories at Black [sic.] schools and compare them to the white schools" (Hawkins, "A Quest" 11). These vast differences are the result of money, or lack thereof, in the case of HBCUs in Mississippi and elsewhere in the country. This becomes more apparent when examining the state appropriations given to these institutions.

State Higher Education Appropriations

According to a report issued by *The Chronicle of Higher Education*, states were expected to spend $42.8 billion on public colleges and financial aid during the 1994-1995 school year. This $1.7 billion increase from the 1993-1994 year only included state tax dollars, not funding from local governments and lotteries. The funding increase has helped many HBCUs, as 16 of these schools saw gains larger than their state averages. Furthermore, the state of Mississippi had the largest gain at 44.8 percent. Nevertheless, this money did not necessarily increase optimism for some Mississippi universities. According to Mississippi's Commissioner of Higher Education, W. Ray Cleere, these gains were not related to *U.S. v. Fordice* and most likely would not have an impact on the proposal to close some state universities (Lively A43, A44).

Even more recently, a study by the Center for Higher Education at Illinois State University showed that states are continuing this trend of channeling more money into their higher educational systems. For instance, during the 1997-1998 fiscal year, state appropriations and student aid reached an all-time high of $49.4 billion. And, during the 1996-1997 and 1995-1996 fiscal years, state higher education funding was approximately $46.5 billion and $44.3 billion, respectively (Schmidt, "State Appropriations" A30; Schmidt, "State Support" A31; "The Nation" 10). Table 5.1 illustrates the total state appropriations for institutions in Kentucky, Mississippi, Ohio and Tennessee in 1995-1996, 1996-1997 and 1997-1998.

Table 5.1: Total State Appropriations for Kentucky, Mississippi, Ohio, and Tennessee, Fiscal Years 1995-1996, 1996-1997 and 1997-1998

	1995-1996	1996-1997	1997-1998
*Kentucky	$677,125,000	$706,655,000	$717,175,000
*Mississippi	659,292,000	669,000,000	727,918,000
*Ohio	1,679,546,000	1,754,923,000	1,863,307,000
*Tennessee	901,253,000	934,487,000	904,670,000

Sources: "The Nation" 10; Schmidt, "State Appropriations" A32; Schmidt, "State Support" A33.

Although most HBCUs do receive an increase in funding on a yearly basis, during 1995-1996 and 1996-1997, 60 percent of public HBCU increases were less than those of their historically white counterparts. Nevertheless, Edward Hines, the Illinois State professor who led the aforementioned research, believed that these decreases did not necessarily indicate any ill will toward HBCUs. Rather, states have merely shifted their spending priorities, a practice that happens annually and often affects other types of state institutions as well. This observation has proven to be correct, as HBCUs saw a change for the better in 1997-1998 (Schmidt, "State Support" A31; Schmidt, "State Appropriations" A31). Tables 5.2-5.4 demonstrate this more in depth. While Table 5.2 shows the funding for Mississippi universities for the 1993-1994 and 1994-1995 fiscal years, Table 5.3 highlights the funding for these same universities (in the thousands only) for the 1996-1997 and 1997-1998 fiscal years only.

Table 5.2: State Appropriations for Mississippi's Public Universities, 1993-1994 and 1994-1995

	1993-1994	1994-1995
*Mississippi State University	$51,782,491	$64,396,751
*University of Mississippi	44,428,295	55,532,560
*University of Southern Mississippi	49,280,235	61,907,638
*Delta State University	12,006,175	19,379,874
*Jackson State University	20,078,936	26,478,362
*Alcorn State University	9,727,636	14,072,727
*Mississippi University for Women	7,357,300	11,202,819
*Mississippi Valley State University	7,030,019	10,244,970

Source: Hawkins, "The Trial" 16.

Table 5.3: 1996-1997 and 1997-1998 State Appropriations for Mississippi's Public Universities (in thousands)		
	1996-1997	**1997-1998**
*Mississippi State University	$116,222	$123,022
*University of Mississippi	167,174	183,416
*University of Southern Mississippi	63,936	68,049
*Delta State University	16,749	18,959
*Jackson State University	28,501	31,558
*Alcorn State University	18,467	20,957
*Mississippi University for Women	12,030	13,186
*Mississippi Valley State University	10,147	11,443

Sources: Schmidt, "State Support" A33; Schmidt, "State Appropriations" A33.

As indicated in both tables, Delta State University, Mississippi University for Women, and the three public black institutions continue to receive a great deal less than the other state schools. Even so, in early 1997, the Mississippi House approved $15 million for the three HBCUs ($5 million per school), as part of the *Fordice* case. This funding will be placed in "The Ayers Endowment Fund," and accrued interest will be applied towards enhancing education and increasing racial diversity. The money will be budgeted from the fiscal 1998 year-end surplus ("Mississippi House" 50).

This trend of providing more funding to the majority universities seems to be the norm for other states as well. The amount of state funding for the other three HBCUs used in this book and one state institution in close proximity (no more than 25 to 30 miles away) to these HBCUs is provided in Table 5.4. The figures are given in the thousands for the 1994-1995, 1996-1997 and 1997-1998 fiscal years. These numbers show a common pattern.

Table 5.4: 1994-1995, 1996-1997 and 1997-1998 State Appropriations (in thousands) for Public HBCUs and One Majority Institution in Kentucky, Ohio, and Tennessee

	HBCU	Majority Institution
*Kentucky	Kentucky State University, Frankfort	University of Kentucky, Lexington
1994-1995	$16,085	$295,481
1996-1997	17,183	319,034
1997-1998	17,504	331,289
*Ohio	Central State University, Wilberforce	Wright State University, Dayton
1994-1995	$12,754	$62,806
1996-1997	13,772	72,041
1997-1998	14,439	74,749
*Tennessee	Tennessee State University, Nashville	Middle Tennessee State University, Murfreesboro
1994-1995	$29,625	$58,600
1996-1997	32,733	64,408
1997-1998	31,724	63,504

Sources: Lively A45, A46; Schmidt, "State Support" A33, A34; Schmidt, "State Appropriations" A32, A33.

Clearly, these numbers indicate that most historically black colleges and universities do not receive as much funding as predominantly white colleges and universities. And, it also should be noted that while both Tennessee State and Central State did not receive the largest amount of funds, they also did not receive the least amount of money in their respective states. Kentucky State University, however, did get the lowest amount of state dollars in Kentucky (Lively A45, A46; Schmidt, "State Support" A33, A34; Schmidt, "State Appropriations" A32, A33). Despite these inequalities in state funding, the federal government is trying to relieve the financial burden of both public and private HBCUs.

Federal Government Support for HBCUs

Under both Clinton Administrations, the federal government has provided more financial support for HBCUs. In fact, on September 21, 1994, the federal government awarded $13 million to 29 historically black colleges and universities. Two of these universities, Kentucky State University and Mississippi Valley State University, received $500,000 each. This money was to be used for the revitalization of the communities and surrounding areas of these universities. In addition, 16 HBCUs, including Central State University, received approximately $4.25 million to study black male violence prevention, drug abuse, and the family. The Energy Department also played an important role in distributing grants to enhance the research capabilities of nine black colleges and universities, including Tennessee State University. The five-year, $1.6 million grants will be used in the environmental sciences ("U.S. Grants" 11; Hawkins, "Sixteen" 10-11; Jaschik, "U.S. Agencies Unveil" A28). Overall, federal aid to historically black institutions for the 1995 education bill, which was approved by Congress in

September 1994, totaled $108.9 million dollars (Dervarics, "HBCUs Get Increase" 5).

Perhaps equally important to the financial sustenance of historically black institutions is the assistance provided by 27 federal departments and agencies. These provisions were mandated in Executive Order 12876, Historically Black Colleges and Universities, and signed by President William J. Clinton on November 1, 1993. Sections 4 and 8 read as follows:

> (*Sec. 4*) To carry out the purposes of this order, each executive department and each agency designated by the Secretary shall, consistent with applicable law, enter into appropriate grants, contracts, or cooperative agreements with historically Black [sic.] colleges and universities. The head of each agency subject to this order shall establish an annual goal for the amount of funds to be awarded in grants, contracts, or cooperative agreements to historically Black [sic.] colleges and universities. Consistent with the funds available to the agency, the goal shall be an amount above the actual amount of such awards from the previous fiscal year and shall represent a substantial effort to increase the amounts available to historically Black [sic.] colleges and universities for grants, contracts, or cooperative agreements. In order to facilitate the attainment of the goals established by this section, the head of each agency subject to this order shall provide technical assistance and information to historically Black [sic.] colleges and universities regarding the program activities of the agency and the preparation of applications or proposals for grants, contracts, or cooperative agreements.

> (*Sec. 8*) The Department of Education, along with other Federal departments or agencies, shall work to encourage the private sector to assist historically Black [sic.] colleges and universities through increased use of such devices and activities as: (1) private sector matching funds to support increased endowments; (2) private sector task forces for institutions in need of assistance; and (3) private sector expertise to facilitate the development of more effective ways to manage finances, improve information management, strengthen facilities, and improve course offerings. These steps will be taken with the goals of enhancing the career prospects of graduates of historically Black [sic.] colleges and universities and increasing the number of such graduates with degrees in science and technology. (White House Initiative 4-5)

Indeed, it is not to be mistaken in these passages that historically black institutions are to be granted special privileges, as many of these same agencies provide assistance for other institutions of higher education as well. In brief, this order merely charges these agencies to put forth a special effort to ensure that HBCUs are not forgotten. This is evident in the awards given to all institutions in fiscal year 1995. For example, out of the $24,296,839,632 total awards, HBCUs were recipients of $1,247,687,479 -- or 5 percent of awarded monies. HBCU-funded projects include: the Department of Agriculture's undergraduate, agriculture/natural resource scholarships to the 17 HBCU land grant institutions, the Department of Health and Human Services' Family and Community Violence Program and technical assistance to Meharry Medical College, the Department of Housing and Urban Development's community development corporation grants, and the Department of Energy's Chairs of Excellence in Engineering, to name a few (The President's Board of Advisors on Historically Black Colleges and Universities, Appendix E, 33-36). And, more recently, three of the universities profiled in this work have received notable awards from federal agencies. Kentucky State received a $500,000, four-year grant from the Department of Health and Human Services to develop a certificate completion program for Head Start Personnel and a $400,000 HUD grant; Tennessee State has been awarded a three-year, $221,000 grant for research activities from the National Institutes of Health; Jackson State was awarded a two-year, $360,000 NASA grant for scholarships for minorities interested in meteorology and physics degrees; and a $400,000 HUD grant (Matthews, "Grants and Awards" 29; "Jackson State University, Jackson State University News" website; Roach 11). The following list provides all of the participating agencies under Executive Order 12876:

- U.S. Department of Agriculture
- U.S. Department of Commerce
- U.S. Department of Defense
- U.S. Department of Education
- U.S. Department of Energy
- U.S. Department of Labor
- U.S. Department of Health and Human Services
- U.S. Department of The Interior
- U.S. Department of Justice
- U.S. Department of Housing and Urban Development
- U.S. Department of State
- U.S. Department of Transportation
- U.S. Department of Treasury
- U.S. Department of Veteran Affairs
- Agency for International Development
- Appalachian Regional Commission
- Central Intelligence Agency
- Environmental Protection Agency
- Equal Employment Opportunity Commission
- National Aeronautics and Space Administration
- National Credit Union Administration
- National Endowment for the Arts
- National Endowment for the Humanities
- National Science Foundation
- Nuclear Regulatory Commission
- Small Business Administration
- United States Information Agency

(Source: *White House Initiative* 10).

Notwithstanding the various forms of assistance provided by the aforementioned federal agencies, there are also several federal grants and/or programs available to historically black colleges and universities to provide supplemental financial support. These programs, referred to as Titles, are a part of the Higher Education Act of 1965 (HEA), reauthorized by the 105th Congress. Consisting of 12 Titles, this legislation is under the Department of Education's jurisdiction and "authorizes the federal government's major student aid programs, as well as other programs providing institutional support and services for disadvantaged students" (Historically Black Colleges and Universities-Educational Testing Service Collaboration 13, 14).

As with other federal assistance programs, there are specific components of the Higher Education Act of 1965 that make provisions for HBCUs and other institutions which serve high minority populations. The most significant of these encompass "Academic and Library and Information Services" (Title II), "Institutional Aid" (Title III), and "Financial Assistance" (Title IV).

Title II - Academic Library and Information Services

The main foci of this program are to enhance college/university libraries by helping them acquire more technologically advanced equipment, continue updating research in information technology, and maintaining and updating the resources in America's largest and most significant research libraries. Subpart D, entitled "Strengthening Library and Information Science Programs and Libraries in Historically Black Colleges and Universities and Other Minority Serving Institutions," enables minority postsecondary institutions to do likewise through grants and/or contracts. Further, it helps in strengthening information science programs and contributing to the number of minority representatives in the library and information science fields (Historically Black Colleges and Universities-Educational Testing Service Collaboration 44).

Title III - Institutional Aid

Title III ensures access to quality higher education for low-income students by providing assistance to those facilities which serve high percentages of minority students. Although Title III consists of three subdivisions, only one of these -- "Part B, Strengthening HBCUs" -- is tailored to HBCUs. This portion provides an opportunity for historically black undergraduate and graduate institutions to improve their academic programs and management, thereby enhancing students' educational experiences. Funds can be used for a variety of purposes, including: purchasing technological equipment (computers, computer accessories, etc.), enriching academic resources, and developing more efficient fiscal management procedures. In 1997, approximately 97 HBCUs were Title III-B recipients, receiving an estimated $108.9 million (Historically Black Colleges and Universities-Educational Testing Service Collaboration 45).

Title IV - Financial Assistance

This is perhaps one of the most crucial programs of the HEA, simply because a significantly high number of African-American students -- nearly 51 percent -- benefit from some form of financial assistance -- Pell Grants, student loans, scholarships, and work study. And, at HBCUs, approximately 90 percent of students are eligible for financial assistance. Pell Grants are available for low-income, undergraduate students and cross racial lines. Closely related to Pell Grants, the Federal Supplemental Education Opportunity Grants (SEOG) are awarded to an institution's neediest students, all of whom are Pell Grant recipients. The Federal Work Study Program is based on financial need as well and provides part-time employment to undergraduate and graduate students either on campus or at governmental agencies or private for-profit and nonprofit organizations (Historically Black Colleges and Universities-Educational Testing Service Collaboration 46-47).

Indeed, all of these initiatives, programs, and grants are critical to the continued survival and sustenance of historically black colleges and universities. Even so, this funding often does not eliminate the dire financial problems and dilapidated physical plants of many HBCUs. And, at any moment, Congressional leaders can decide to drastically reduce or increase allocations in specific education-related areas. Federal support for higher education programs, and especially those which impact HBCUs, are subject to the moods and whims of Congress. Thus, HBCU administrators, alumni, employees, and students can not afford to ignore the financial future of these educational institutions.

References

Book(s)

Thompson, Daniel C. "Black College Faculty and Students: The Nature of Their Interaction." *Black Colleges in America: Challenge, Development, Survival*. Eds. Charles V. Willie and Ronald R. Edmonds. New York: Teachers College Press, 1978. 180-194.

Periodicals

Dervarics, Charles. "HBCUs Get Increase In Final 1995 Spending Bill." *Black Issues In Higher Education* 20 Oct. 1994: 5.

Hawkins, B. Denise. "A Quest for Equality." *Black Issues In Higher Education* 5 May 1994: 10-13.

_____. "Sixteen HBCUs Awarded $4 Million to Study Black Male Violence Prevention." *Black Issues In Higher Education* 6 Oct. 1994: 10-11.

_____. "The Trial: Round Two for *Fordice* Mississippi Higher Education Back in Court." *Black Issues In Higher Education* 2 June 1994: 12-16.

Jaschik, Scott. "U. S. Agencies Unveil New Support for Historically Black Colleges." *The Chronicle of Higher Education* 12 Oct. 1994: A28.

Lively, Kit. "$42.8-Billion for Public Colleges: State Appropriations for Fiscal 1994-95 Show Biggest Increase Since Recession Began." *The Chronicle of Higher Education* 19 Oct. 1994: A43-A46.

Matthews, Maya. "Grants & Awards." *Black Issues In Higher Education* 4 Sept. 1997: 29.

_____. "Grants & Awards." *Black Issues In Higher Education* 30 Oct. 1997: 29.

"Mississippi House Agrees to Set Aside $15 Million for Historically Black Universities." *Black Issues In Higher Education* 20 Feb. 1997: 50.

"The Nation." *The Chronicle of Higher Education Almanac.*" 2 Sept. 1996: 10.

Roach, Ronald. "Working Capitol Hill: Presidents of Historically Black Institutions Spend Week in Washington, Where HUD Grants $6.5 Million to Seventeen HBCUs." *Black Issues In Higher Education* 16 Oct. 1997: 10-11.

Schmidt, Peter. "State Appropriations for Colleges Increase at Highest Rate Since 1990." *The Chronicle of Higher Education* 14 Nov. 1997: A30-A33.

_____. "State Support for Higher Education Shows Largest Percentage Increase Since 1990." *The Chronicle of Higher Education* 1 Nov. 1996: A31-A35.

"U.S. Grants $13 Million to Rebuild Areas Around Black Colleges." *Black Issues In Higher Education* 6 Oct. 1994: 11.

Miscellaneous

Historically Black Colleges and Universities-Educational Testing Service Collaboration. *Higher Education Act Reauthorization: A Handbook for Historically Black Colleges and Universities.* Princeton, NJ: Feb. 1997.

"Jackson State University, Jackson State University News." *Jackson State University* website. Internet WWW page at: <http://ccaix.jsums.edu/~www/jsunews.htm> (last updated 12 Nov. 1997).

The President's Board of Advisors on Historically Black Colleges and Universities. *A Century of Success: Historically Black Colleges and Universities, America's National Treasure.* 1995-1996 Annual Report. Washington: Sept. 1996.

White House Initiative on Historically Black Colleges and Universities. *Making A Difference for Historically Black Colleges and Universities (Executive Order 12876).* Brochure. Washington: U.S. Department of Education, 1996.

White House Initiative on Historically Black Colleges and Universities. Pamphlet. Washington: GPO.

Through exploration of each individual history of the six universities highlighted here, this chapter provides background information, enrollment patterns, brief academic program descriptions, graduate numbers, and faculty and student ethnic breakdown. Updated statistics and information obtained in interviews is included on each school, with the exception being Central State University. *For comparison purposes, please refer to Chapter Four for recent, approximate enrollment figures and graduate numbers*. Due to the university's recent legal struggles and the inability to obtain more current information, the information in this section reflects the university's status during the 1994-1995 academic year, when the interview was conducted.

Central State University

Ohio's only state-funded historically black university, Central State University is located in Wilberforce, Ohio, about 18 miles from Dayton. Central State University is proud of its legacy, in "having produced thousands of well-prepared, well-educated students who might not have otherwise received any higher education at all" (*Central State University 1992-1994 Catalog* 10, 11). With a multipurpose mission, Central State strives for academic excellence (teaching, research, and service), prepares students with a background in liberal arts and technology, preserves African-American heritage, and encourages self-edification through nurturing and support systems (*CSU 1992-1994 Catalog* 10).

Central State's roots are at Wilberforce University, Ohio's only private HBCU, located across the street from Central State. In 1887, the Ohio General Assembly passed an act which would provide for the creation of a Combined Normal and Industrial Department at Wilberforce. Although located on Wilberforce's campus, the department was still considered a separate entity and had its own Board of Trustees. During the 1940s, Central State was transformed again. In 1941, the department was called the College of Education and Industrial Arts and in 1947, the institution broke away, becoming Wilberforce State College. After being named Central State College, the university received its present name in November 1965 (*CSU 1992-1994 Catalog* 10-11).

The academic disciplines are divided into five colleges (subject to change with the new stipulations, as reported in Chapter Four), and the students can choose from 33 majors. Among other affiliations, Central State is accredited by the North Central Association of Colleges and Schools. Also, Central State University is known for its research and service commitments, as seen in some of its programs. They include Urban Literacy, Education and Support Services, Manufacturing Engineering, Water Resource Management, and International Affairs (*CSU 1992-1994 Catalog* 10, 11).

Central State's enrollment was down during the 1994-1995 academic year. Donald K. Anthony, former director of public relations and alumni affairs at the university, attributed this to a decrease in high school graduates and an inability of many high school students to pass Ohio's Proficiency Test (a test given to all Ohio high school students and a determining factor in whether the student graduates). Thus, "the marketplace is down." In the 1994-1995 academic year, the enrollment was slightly under 2,700 as opposed to 1993-1994 when the enrollment was slightly under 3,000. During the 1994 Annual Spring Commencement, Central State University awarded degrees to 424 students, a record for the university.♦ Approximately one-half of these graduates received degrees in some aspect of business.

As for diversity at the university, Anthony responded that the non-African-American student population is usually between 8 and 10 percent and about 28 percent of the administration and faculty is Caucasian. Forty-seven percent of the student body is comprised of African-American males. When asked whether the state had established goals regarding other race students, Anthony responded: "Nobody has really pushed us, forced us, or encouraged us to have more nontraditional students. There's probably a reason for that -- they [the state] probably don't [doesn't] want them here and would rather they go somewhere else. We haven't gotten to that point yet."

Tennessee State University

Located in Nashville, Tennessee, Tennessee State University is the only public, four-year historically black university in the state. The university prides itself on being "committed to educating a non-racially identifiable student body" (*Tennessee State University 1993-1995 Undergraduate Catalog* 1). In its 87 years of existence, Tennessee State has endured many changes.

Established as a land-grant institution, Tennessee State University was originally known as the Agricultural and Industrial State Normal School when it opened on June 19, 1912. Ten years later, the school became known as a four-year teacher's college, and in 1924, the school's name changed to Agricultural and Industrial State Normal College. In 1946, Tennessee State was accredited by the Southern Association of Colleges and Schools. In 1951, it was granted university status and became a "full-fledged land-grant university" in 1958. The university received its present name in 1968 (Whitfield). During February 1977, Judge Frank Gray ordered the merger of the University of Tennessee at Nashville and Tennessee State University. This merger was finalized on July 1, 1979. Presently, Tennessee State consists of two campuses -- the main campus (in north Nashville) and the downtown campus, formerly known as UT Nashville and now called The Avon N. Williams, Jr. campus. The School of Business and Evening Program are located at this site (*TSU 1993-1995 Undergraduate Catalog* 4, 6).

In its mission statement, Tennessee State is classified as a "land-grant, urban and comprehensive" university. This simply means that the university not only has agricultural and research programs which allow it to function in a land-grant capacity, but also provides wide programming in other areas such as education, business, and nursing, which serve the comprehensive function. As an urban university, it offers programs and a curriculum -- degree and non-degree programs; day, evening, and weekend classes -- that tailor to the needs of a working population. Even more important, the university is committed to serving all students, regardless of race, traditional/nontraditional status, and commuter/residential status. With this in mind, Tennessee State also strives to help those who may be educationally, culturally, or socioeconomically disadvantaged. Its motto is "Think, Work, Serve" (*TSU 1993-1995 Undergraduate Catalog* 4).

Tennessee State University's academic curriculum is comprised of seven schools, which offer 41 undergraduate degrees. At present, the university has a limited graduate program. Although master's degrees are offered in several fields of study, doctoral degrees are awarded only in

Education and Public Administration (*TSU 1993-1995 Undergraduate Catalog* 4, 11). Yet, despite limited graduate programs, Tennessee State's research programs serve as some of the university's strong points. For example, the Center of Excellence and Information Systems Management operates a satellite in California, which processes robotics information. And, the Biological Research Programs are exploring health issues like AIDS and hypertension (Qualls-Brooks).

With a commitment to diversity, Tennessee State has taken steps to ensure that this promise is kept. For example, Minority Student Affairs provides financial aid and registration assistance to Caucasian undergraduate students. The role of Minority Student Affairs is to see that the university is aware of and sensitive to the needs of its minority students (*TSU 1993-1995 Undergraduate Catalog* 35).

During the 1996-1997 academic year, Tennessee State University continued to embrace and move toward a diverse population. Of the 8,608 students enrolled during the fall of 1996, approximately 68 percent were African American, 28 percent Caucasian, and 4 percent other. Further, the faculty for this same year was almost 55 percent non-African American. These numbers are being closely monitored by the state and must be in accordance with those objectives established under the Stipulation of Settlement agreement. Academically, the university is making advancements, as 1,373 students graduated in the spring and summer of 1997. The four most popular fields were the Arts and Sciences, Nursing, Engineering, and Business divisions (Qualls-Brooks).

Although the university is striving for diversity, according to the 1994-1995 Student Government president, the campus environment was still tense and segregated. At Tennessee State University, the majority of the Caucasian undergraduates, who made up about 28 percent of the student body, were nontraditional students -- older, married, and commuters. Therefore, very few -- only about 19 out of 2,000 campus residents -- lived on campus. Dixon was straightforward and honest, saying that students usually socialized with their peers who were from the same ethnic or racial background. Students commingled mainly in class. Further, in most cases, students had good relationships with the faculty, who were more integrated (as far as percentages) than the student body.

Kentucky State University

> At KSU we're proud of the diversity of our students, and we believe that our University benefits greatly from the myriad of personalities, backgrounds, and values that they embody. . . . Only at KSU can you study at a historically Black [sic.] university that offers the warmth of a smaller setting, while meeting young people from all areas of the world, who bring to KSU fresh faces, knowledge and ideologies. (*KS You: A Portrait* 1)

Kentucky State University not only strives to preserve its cultural heritage, but does so in the midst of diversity. Located in Frankfort, approximately 25 miles from Lexington, Kentucky State is the smallest public university and also the only public HBCU in Kentucky. The university is a liberal studies institution that incorporates multicultural education in its curriculum (*Kentucky State University Catalogue, 1994-1996* 12, 13). Once a predominantly black campus, the student body and faculty composition no longer reflect this. In the fall of 1996, the enrollment was 2,356, slightly lower than the fall 1994 enrollment of 2,500, the highest in the university's history (Peale; *KSU in Brief, Fall 1996*). According to *KSU in Brief, Fall*

1996, the student body was approximately 43 percent Caucasian, 53 percent African American, and 4 percent other (Asian, Native American, and Hispanic). The faculty members were 57 percent white, 34 percent black, and 9 percent Asian (*KSU in Brief, Fall 1996*). Although Peale and Bunton-Douglas, the alumni affairs director and staff writer, respectively, were unable to give specific numbers and goals, they did say these percentages were in compliance with set goals established by the state.

As with Tennessee State, although the student body at Kentucky State is diversified, African-American and Caucasian students rarely socialized outside of class (Coleman). Coleman, the 1994-1995 Student Government president, described the classroom relationships as basic tolerance, with everyone wanting to "guard his or her own territory." In common with Tennessee State, most of the Caucasian students were nontraditional -- state government employees and part-time. Thus, they were rarely involved in the social scene on campus. Because of this, many African-American students resented their presence: "Black students say that white students 'rape' the university. They come to the school, use its facilities, go to class, and go home. They don't contribute [back] to the university by supporting events" (Coleman). Coleman also said that in the cafeteria, the black faculty eat with each other and the white faculty eat with each other. Faculty and student relationships were fine on the whole. However, some African-American students in the Psychology and Liberal Arts departments had difficulty with the white faculty members because of the Westernized curriculum.

Now known as a small comprehensive university, Kentucky State has changed since its early beginnings in May 1886 as the State Normal School for Colored Persons. The original purpose of the school was to train black teachers for Kentucky's black school districts. After the 1890 Land Grant Act, the school became a land-grant university, offering courses in home economics, agriculture, and mechanics. In 1893, a high school was established. These transitional stages became commonplace for the school. Keeping in line with other HBCUs, Kentucky State University underwent several name changes before choosing its current name in 1972. In 1902, 1926, 1938, and 1952, the school changed its name -- Kentucky Normal and Industrial Institute for Colored Persons, Kentucky State Industrial College for Colored Persons, Kentucky State College for Negroes, and Kentucky State College, respectively (*KSU Catalogue, 1994-1996* 12).

Kentucky State offers associate degrees in six disciplines, bachelor's degrees in 30, and a master's degree in Public Administration. In the spring of 1997, approximately 300 students received degrees from Kentucky State. Many were in nursing, computer science, criminal justice, biology, business, social work, and education. The university is accredited by the Southern Association of Colleges and Schools ("Kentucky State University 1996-1997 Graduation Report;" *KSU Catalogue, 1994-1996* 6).

Living up to its research and community service obligations, the university founded the Center of Excellence for the Study of Kentucky African-Americans in 1993. Its mission is to provide information about Kentucky African Americans, all African Americans, and African heritage. The Community Research Service helps find solutions to agricultural, economic, and social issues facing Kentucky citizens, especially those who live in rural areas. This serves the university's land grant responsibility. And, the National Center for Diversity, founded in October 1992, is a network of Cooperative Extension Programs which includes Kentucky State, the University of Wisconsin, Pennsylvania State University, and the U.S. Department of Agriculture. This consortium provides resources that encourage respect, cooperation, and appreciation among diverse peoples (*KSU Catalogue, 1994-1996* 14, 79, 80).

Alcorn State University

Alcorn State University, founded in 1871, was the first historically black land-grant institution. The university was named for former Mississippi Governor James Alcorn, who suggested that the state legislature lend financial support to the institution. Like other universities, Alcorn's name has been changed. In 1878, Alcorn University became Alcorn A&M College. Almost a century later, in 1974, the institution's name changed once more to Alcorn State University. The university is in Lorman, about 80 miles from Jackson (*Alcorn State University* Brochure).

In addition to graduate degrees offered in education, agriculture, and science, the 42 undergraduate academic programs fall within five divisions: Agriculture and Applied Sciences, Arts and Sciences, Business, Education and Psychology, and Nursing (*ASU* Brochure). And, in May 1997, 521 students graduated, mainly with degrees in secondary education, nursing, and biology. Alcorn State is accredited by the Southern Association of Colleges and Schools and other associations as well. More than 2,700 students attended the university during the 1996-1997 academic year (Payne).

Alcorn State's student body and faculty are predominantly African American. In the fall of 1996, the student body was 95 percent African American, 4 percent Caucasian, and 1 percent Asian/Hispanic. Although more evenly distributed, the faculty was 61 percent African American, 24 percent Caucasian, and 15 percent Asian/Hispanic. Despite these numbers, Anthony, the 1994-1995 Student Government Association (Acting) President painted a picture of racial harmony at Alcorn State University. In fact, he characterized the university as "one big, happy family," and stated there was not discrimination and the "whites fit right in." Although there are no established goals, the state has suggested that Alcorn increase its minority enrollment (Payne).

Mississippi Valley State University

Proclaiming that it can provide an excellent education to all students -- "those who can move at an accelerated pace, students who have adequate prior preparation, and students who are educationally deficient in their prior preparation" -- Mississippi Valley State University operates on the same premise as all HBCUs. That is, it can take any student, regardless of socioeconomic and academic constraints, and create a success story. Mississippi Valley is in the Mississippi Delta (Itta Bena), one of the most economically deprived areas of the state and nation. Despite this disadvantage, the university is committed to teaching, research activities, and public service in the surrounding community (*Mississippi Valley State University General Catalog 1994-1996* 12).

Unlike most HBCUs, Mississippi Valley State University has only been around since 1946, when the Mississippi Legislature passed legislation for the establishment of the university. The initial purpose of Mississippi Vocational College was to train teachers and provide vocational instruction. The institution did not open until 1950. Along with a name change in 1964 to Mississippi Valley State College, the institution began to offer degrees in the liberal arts, science, and education. In 1974, the institution was granted university status (*MVSU Catalog 1994-1996* 10, 11).

The academic curriculum is divided into 13 departments and offers 22 majors with additional emphases in these areas. Also, there are master's degrees offered in Environmental Health and Criminal Justice. Mississippi Valley State University is a member of the Southern Association of Colleges and Schools (*MVSU Catalog 1994-1996* 1, 9, 215; "MS Valley" 46).

Mississippi Valley State University is the smallest of the three Mississippi HBCUs. According to the Information Services Coordinator Wanda R. Young, Mississippi Valley had about 2,192 students enrolled in the spring of 1997. Approximately 2 percent and 35 percent of the student body and faculty, respectively, was non-African American during the fall 1996. As with Alcorn State, Walker, the student body representative, said there were not any racial problems among the Caucasian, African-American, Ethiopian, or Middle Eastern students. In addition, Young said she had not heard of any set goals established by the state to change these percentages. The smaller student body population is reflected in the number of graduates -- 277 -- in the spring of 1997. The majors with the highest number of graduates included criminal justice, social work, elementary education, biology, and business administration (Young).

Jackson State University

Mississippi's only urban university, Jackson State University has been educating African Americans since 1877. As a comprehensive university, Jackson State focuses its research and service on those problems and issues ailing metropolitan centers such as Jackson, home of Jackson State, and other cities in the country and the world (*Jackson State University* Brochure 1).

Jackson State University was established by the American Baptist Home Mission Society. The first baccalaureate degree was awarded in 1924 (Roebuck and Murty 74). Accredited by the Southern Association of Colleges and Schools, the university offers over 100 undergraduate and graduate areas of study. Doctoral degrees are offered in Early Childhood Education, Environmental Science, and Public Administration. Jackson State is the only HBCU that has an undergraduate program in meteorology. In addition to having a University College and Academic Skills Center, which make the transition to college life easier, there are workshops on study skills, time management, and tutorial programs. And, for top students, there is the W.E.B. DuBois Honors College (*JSU* Brochure 2, 3, 6-7, 17).

During the 1996-1997 academic year, there were approximately 6,218 students attending Jackson State and more than 300 faculty members. While 97 percent of these students was African American, 0.9 percent Caucasian, and 2 percent other, close to 32 percent of the faculty was non-African American. There have been no established state goals to alter these percentages. In the spring of 1996, Jackson State awarded degrees to approximately 576 students. Many of these degrees were from the Schools of Science and Technology, Education, Liberal Arts, and Business ("Jackson State University, Institutional Research and Planning" website). Like other public HBCUs that are adjusting to diversity, the university is "proud of its heritage as an HBCU, committed to its future as a diversified institution, and dedicated to developing individual students and solving urban problems" (*JSU* Brochure 17).

At Press Time:

♦**During the June 1998 Central State Commencement Exercises, 283 students received their degrees (Fisher, "Efforts Pay" 6A).**

References

Book(s)

Roebuck, Julian B., and Komanduri S. Murty. *Historically Black Colleges and Universities: Their Place in American Higher Education.* Westport, CT: Praeger Publishers, 1993.

Periodicals

Fisher, Mark. "Efforts Pay Off at CSU." *Dayton Daily News* 8 Aug. 1998: 1A, 6A.

"MS Valley State to Offer New Academic Programs." *Black Issues In Higher Education* 11 July 1996: 46.

Interviews

Anthony, Donald K. Director of Public Relations and Alumni Affairs, Central State University. Personal interview. 1 Feb. 1995.

Anthony, Mark. Student Government Association Acting President, Alcorn State University. Telephone interview. 3 Mar. 1995.

Bunton-Douglas, Kimberly. Staff Writer, Kentucky State University. Personal interview. 21 Feb. 1995.

Coleman, Michele. Student Government Association President, Kentucky State University. Personal interview. 21 Feb. 1995.

Dixon, Angela M. Student Government Association President, Tennessee State University. Personal interview. 15 Feb. 1995.

Payne, Ralph L. Director of University Relations, Alcorn State University. Telephone interview. 8 Mar. 1995.

_____. Director of University Relations, Alcorn State University. Questionnaire. 7 Oct. 1997.

Peale, Kathy O. Director of Alumni Affairs, Kentucky State University. Personal interview. 21 Feb. 1995.

Qualls-Brooks, Phyllis. Director of Public Relations, Tennessee State University. Personal interview. 16 Feb. 1995.

_____. Director of Public Relations, Tennessee State University. Questionnaire.

20 Aug. 1997.

Walker, Marcus. Student Government Association Member, Mississippi Valley State University. Telephone interview. 3 Mar. 1995.

Whitfield, Margaret C. Director of Alumni Relations, Tennessee State University. Personal interview. 16 Feb. 1995.

Young, Wanda R. Information Services Coordinator, Mississippi Valley State University. Questionnaire. 28 July 1997.

Miscellaneous

Alcorn State University. Brochure. Lorman, MS: Alcorn State University Office of Admissions.

Central State University 1992-1994 Catalog. Wilberforce, OH: Central State University.

Jackson State University. Brochure. Jackson, MS: Jackson State University Office of Admissions.

"Jackson State University, Institutional Research and Planning." *Jackson State University* website. Internet WWW page at: <http://ccaix.jsums.edu/instres/> (last updated 4 Apr. 1997).

Kentucky State University Catalogue, 1994-1996. Frankfort: Kentucky State University.

"Kentucky State University 1996-1997 Graduation Report." Table. Frankfort: Kentucky State University, 1997.

KSU in Brief, Fall 1996. Brochure. Frankfort: Kentucky State University Institutional Research and Planning, Office for Policy Management.

KS You: A Portrait! Brochure. Frankfort: Kentucky State University Office of Admissions.

Mississippi Valley State University General Catalog 1994-1996. Itta Bena, MS: Mississippi Valley State University.

Tennessee State University 1993-1995 Undergraduate Catalog. Nashville: Tennessee State University.

In examining where each university is in relation to coping with integration, the interview responses demonstrate that universities which have been implementing public relations plans and state-mandated integration goals for some time have more fully developed survival plans and strategies. On the other hand, those universities which have been affected most recently by integration demands have survival plans which are more limited in scope. Despite differing plans, respondents were on one accord about preserving their institutions and all HBCUs. They offered strong, passionate, and candid opinions about those issues affecting African-American higher education and refused to apologize for their feelings and lack of "political correctness." Their comments are real, sensitive, emotional, and at times, harsh. *The interview questions are located in Appendix E.* (*Please note that the responses are recorded as they were stated in the 1995 interviews and reflect the staff or respondents' elected positions at that time. Statements have not been altered, albeit three interviewees' names have been modified. An asterisk denotes these changes.*)

The Role of HBCUs in Higher Education and the African-American Community

Black college advocates are unwavering in their belief in HBCUs' multifaceted purposes -- serving and meeting the economic, cultural, educational, and social needs of their students and the African-American community. The majority of respondents were no different, agreeing that HBCUs serve an invaluable function in both the American educational system and African-American community. The general consensus was that these institutions were founded expressly for the education of African Americans and continue to educate mostly African Americans. They are quality institutions producing quality graduates who are not only competent, but also possess the ability to make many outstanding contributions to society.

Central State University

Donald K. Anthony, the public relations and alumni affairs director at Central State, responded that in the past, HBCUs provided an education for African Americans when they could not go anywhere else, and today these schools are very much needed as they contribute to the "upward mobility" of African Americans. This important role is quite visible in the fact the "HBCUs still graduate 25 to 30 percent of all African Americans throughout the country." He expressed the image of HBCUs as quality and professional institutions which are able to successfully compete with other institutions of higher learning:

> We are not second-class, although we may be treated or viewed as second-class. There's nothing second-class about Ben Chavis or Jesse Jackson. These people came out of HBCUs and made their mark nationally. The image we're trying to get across is that we might be smaller and have limited resources, but our products can compete with anybody in the world.

From a cultural and social standpoint, Anthony described HBCUs as an extension of the African-American family. He felt those nurturing qualities and teaching methods that are the HBCUs' "forte," will definitely be sacrificed if diversity and accommodating non-black students become commonplace. In other words, the family-like atmosphere is not found at the majority institutions.

Tennessee State University

Describing the significance of HBCUs, the Alumni Relations Director Margaret C. Whitfield stated: "They were there when no one else was; we need to continue in this vital role because we provide our own with what other institutions can not and never will." Attorney Robert L. Smith, the vice president of the Tennessee State University National Alumni Association, echoed similar sentiments. According to Smith, these schools provided former slaves with an education that enabled them to become self-sufficient in society. Presently, the universities serve the same purpose as any other university, except they "bring out the very best in African-American individuals" by educating in a manner that historically white institutions may not be able to do.

In a much-related vein, all five Tennessee State University respondents expressed similar feelings about the image of all HBCUs and Tennessee State in particular. Above all, one word that was frequently used to describe HBCUs was "quality." The director of public relations, Phyllis Qualls-Brooks, said Tennessee State graduates epitomize quality in all facets of the professional arena, from elementary school teachers to talk show host and business entrepreneur Oprah Winfrey. In addition, Smith and Lawrence E. Porter, former Tennessee State University National Alumni Association president, said while Tennessee State has been and still is committed to educating African Americans, it is not limited to serving only African Americans, but reaches out to all people: "TSU is probably the most integrated school in the state of Tennessee right now and it takes its responsibility for educating a diverse population very seriously. It is doing that recognizing that it has a responsibility to the black community and black students" (Porter).

Closely aligned with this image was also the notion that the unique nurturing qualities and teaching methods of HBCUs would not be lost with diversity and adapting to non-black students. This response was quite different from the stance taken by Central State's Anthony, who commented that the teaching methods and nurturing qualities would be lost with integration. The feeling was that other diverse groups of people would benefit from this nurturing as well, for this is not a quality that can easily be turned on or off according to an ethnic group (Porter; Whitfield). In addition, Whitfield commented that the caring and nurturing atmosphere of HBCUs is contributing to the influx of black students returning to HBCUs because they are not exposed to this at predominantly white universities.

Kentucky State University

For Michele Coleman, 1994-1995 Student Government Association president, Kentucky State University has given her many opportunities that would not have been available to her at a majority institution: "HBCUs provide a more conducive environment and give a sense of home and an opportunity to prosper." Building on this perspective, Kathy O. Peale, the alumni affairs director, and Staff Writer Kimberly Bunton-Douglas, commented that contrary to popular belief, HBCUs are not partying schools or, as Peale said, "a bed for kids who are not well-prepared."

Indeed, these schools remain strong academically, the students are well-rounded, and politically aware (Bunton-Douglas). Peale reemphasized the same position as Central State's Anthony on the continued existence of these schools, stating that historically black colleges and universities still graduate a significant number of African Americans. Therefore, they play a vital role in society. When asked whether nurturing qualities and teaching methods will be diminished in an effort to achieve diversity, both Peale and Bunton-Douglas responded "no." Nevertheless, Coleman felt otherwise, saying this is a matter that will depend on other factors, namely enrollment patterns and the university's hiring practices of faculty.

Alcorn State University

Of the 15 interviewees from the six universities who gave their views on the multiple purpose of HBCUs, the university relations director and the Student Government Association acting president (1994-1995) at Alcorn State had replies which differed from the standard explanations. Ralph L. Payne, the university relations director, said that these universities are no different than any other universities -- to provide an education to all who aspire. However, he did note that HBCUs differ on one account, which is to maintain a level of sensitivity to the needs of black students and a support base for them. Student Government Association (Acting) President Mark Anthony's interpretation differed:

> I think that black students attend black institutions in order to not stray too far away from their own cultural heritage. When some people go to predominantly white universities, they somewhat lose a little bit of themselves. At a black university, you are with your people; whereas, at a white university, you're trying to mingle and do certain things to make yourself fit in.

In like manner, the two representatives also differed in their descriptions of the images of HBCUs. Payne's stance echoed the other respondents at the sample universities -- HBCUs are excellent institutions that "produce quality students who are able to do whatever they are hired to do and do so in a manner that would bring credit back to the university." Giving a more egalitarian answer, Anthony simply stated that HBCUs are no better or worse than any of the majority institutions, but all institutions are equal and have imperfections.

In speaking on the nurturing qualities and teaching methods unique to HBCUs, Anthony provided the most profound and powerful perspective. Deviating from the norm once again, he believed these qualities will be lost if HBCUs diversify and cater to non-black students. According to Anthony, there are vast differences in the teaching methods of white and black professors: "Certain things I have learned from my black instructors, I never learned from the white instructors."

Mississippi Valley State University

While Student Government Association member (1994-1995), Marcus Walker,* offered the common definition of HBCUs as institutions set up to educate and suit the needs of black students, he also expounded on the meaning of "historically black." It means these institutions are to be administered by black administrators, presidents, deans, and faculty heads. In addition, the Information Services Coordinator Wanda R. Young contributed further to Walker's definition as she focused on the image of HBCUs as universities committed to extending higher educational opportunities for all, for she stated:

> I would like for the public to know, and the universities to project that we are all working together for the same cause. We're all here to educate and provide a quality education for the young people who come through our doors. The same goes for Mississippi Valley -- we are a quality institution, we have done very well with the resources we have had, and we plan to be here on into the twenty-first century.

Once again, the notion of losing teaching methods and the nurturing atmosphere of HBCUs if diversity and assimilation become widespread, received mixed comments from Mississippi Valley representatives. Deirdre Baldwin,* an alumni relations representative, did not foresee a problem with diversifying, for she stated: "For some strange reason, we [African Americans] can teach non-blacks, but non-blacks can not teach blacks as well or effectively as blacks can." On the contrary, Young believed that diversity and accommodating other race students may forfeit these qualities; yet, this would depend upon who was in control of these institutions. If HBCUs were controlled by Caucasian males, then much of the caring environment would be lost.

Jackson State University

Jackson State University's Public Information Representative Rochelle Neal,* like other interviewees, was adamant about the role of HBCUs both in the past and the present -- to provide a meaningful educational experience for African Americans. From her standpoint, it does not matter that other universities exist. What is relevant is that HBCUs serve an invaluable function in the African-American community today. HBCUs are doing what other universities can not: "Hard data show that they [the majority institutions] are not preparing our young people. I also think the point should be made that HBCUs, like all other schools, have their own points of uniqueness and strengths, and they should be judged on those merits." And, consistent with many other responses, especially Tennessee State interviewees, Neal expressed that HBCUs are about nurturing because they have to be. This can not and will not be relinquished if HBCUs diversify and meet the needs of non-black populations.

Integration versus Desegregation

In the American educational system, the words desegregation and integration have been used interchangeably. Webster's Ninth New Collegiate Dictionary defines desegregation as "the act of freeing any law, provision, or practice requiring isolation of the members of a particular race," and integration as "incorporation as equals into society." These words have very similar meanings, but should they be used synonymously when applied to higher education? Many of the interviewees didn't think so. This section explores how the respondents interpreted these terms.

Central State University

Taking a historical perspective, Anthony defined integration in the context of the 1960s. From his viewpoint, integration was both a help and a hindrance. The positive result was that African Americans were able to make many gains and were finally given the freedom of choice in where to reside, work, and attend college. Nevertheless, with integration there was also assimilation and a loss of African-American heritage, for he commented that "we lost a lot of our culture, our support base, and our getting it done on our own." He associated segregation with educational opportunities, or the lack thereof: "People should have the option to go to a historically black college or university, but many people look upon them as segregated schools. African-American institutions have never been segregated by choice. If we're segregated, it's through default."

Tennessee State University

Since 1968 (the beginning of the *Geier* case), the meanings of integration and desegregation have become more than just mere words on the printed page, but rather a reality for Tennessee State University. The two interviewees who are most active with the National Alumni Association, Smith and Porter, provided the most comprehensive explanation. According to Smith, the distinction between desegregation and integration can be observed in their outcomes. Whereas integration is associated with historically white institutions, desegregation is applied to HBCUs. In short, integration has served to edify white institutions and desegregation has virtually destroyed and eliminated the history of black institutions:

> As it relates to white institutions, integration becomes the addition or access to some degree of citizens of color to what was a historically white institution. When you get to African-American institutions, desegregation seems to take on some notion of not integration, meaning white citizens coming into a formerly black setting and having access. It seems to be the elimination of the historical black presence and transitioning into a majority white presence with black citizens in attendance.

However, Porter provided a more political response, labeling desegregation as more of a legal remedy in which the government requires a balance between the races and sexes in order to rectify past injustices. Integration is a moral issue, or "the bringing together of people because that's the way society works and that's the way the system is."

Kentucky State University

Kentucky State interviewees' explanations were less analytical and more brief and concise. Peale perceived integration in higher education as people of all backgrounds and races uniting and being educated together, while desegregation is the implementation of objectives and goals that require certain percentages of other race people in faculty, staff, and administrative levels at HBCUs. Adding a differing angle to this definition, Bunton-Douglas described desegregation as "forced integration," and integration as a voluntary process.

Alcorn State University

Expressing a combination of viewpoints stated by Central State University's Anthony and Tennessee State University's Smith, Payne said that although HBCUs were legally mandated to be segregated at one time, black schools have never denied access to anyone; their doors have always been open to whoever wanted to attend. Even so, the concept of integration, when applied to historically black institutions, takes on a new connotation with more complex implications. Dubbing this "submersion," Payne stated: "I view integration as an open opportunity for all, but in most instances with the historically black institutions, where integration is taking place, they've [HBCUs] been submerged into a situation that didn't open everything up for everyone."

Mississippi Valley State University

Baldwin provided another aspect of integration and desegregation. Using the history of Mississippi's higher educational system as her example, she stated that at times there was no distinction between these concepts. But, more often than not, this was not the case, as universities used programs and course offerings to limit access and opportunities for students. Integration means the coming together as one, but this unification failed to happen in Mississippi higher education: "In higher education, there were still some schools that were predominantly black because of course offerings. They were still segregated, not integrated. If all universities would have had the major course offerings, there would've been a real integrated system." This view echoed the Supreme Court's ruling in *U.S. v. Fordice* that course offerings were duplicated at both black and white Mississippi universities, thereby contributing to institutions as either predominantly white or black.

Jackson State University

Neal,* of Jackson State University, reiterated the same stance as Baldwin of Mississippi Valley. Moreover, she defined both concepts in relation to the *Ayers* case (*U.S. v. Fordice*), which said Mississippi universities had not integrated. She said that desegregation does not necessarily bring about integration and vice-versa. In other words, Jackson State may have Caucasian students and Ole' Miss (University of Mississippi), Mississippi State University, and the other predominantly white institutions may have black students, but that does not truly mean that a university is integrated. "I think you have to look at more than the words and whether or not there exists the capability of a student attending a certain university," Neal said.

The HBCU Image, Preserving Cultural Heritage and Diversifying

Will it be possible for HBCUs to preserve their cultural heritage if forced to incorporate another culture's viewpoint and history? The respondents answered this by refuting the perceived image of HBCUs as inferior and worthless, and the notion that integration will improve this. Also, they addressed their concerns about safeguarding the identity of HBCUs and maintaining African-American control over these institutions if integration is implemented across the board.

Central State University

Using other HBCUs which have integrated as the basis for his argument, Anthony stated that integration has not really improved how outsiders view and label HBCUs as mediocre and inadequate institutions of higher learning. Even more important, he stated that integration efforts may threaten the continued existence of these universities as historically black. He said losses will be observed in the lack of African-American administrative power and the universities will no longer have separate identities. "When integration happens, Central State becomes a part of

Ohio State or Wright State. We're very concerned about that and we're hoping and praying that doesn't happen. But, if we were willing to change some things and maybe give up control, possibly some of our money problems would go away." Further, he implied that one must look at the fact that all public institutions are not operating on an equal funding level, meaning many HBCUs receive a lesser amount of money than their white counterparts. He noted that whenever there is a shortage of state funds, the remedy is to close the minority (HBCU) institutions.

Above all, Anthony mentioned that African-American students will be affected the most by integration efforts, as they will no longer have any control over their educational destinies. Central State University has operated under an open enrollment policy, in which students were admitted regardless of their grade point averages. Anthony believed that if integration or a merger occurs, this policy will be discontinued, and many African-American students will not have an opportunity to receive a higher education because they will not be accepted elsewhere. Nevertheless, Anthony did say that integration may have one positive impact by providing an opportunity for Central State to increase funding, upgrade facilities, and attract the top African-American and Caucasian students. As an example, he cited the competition that exists between Central State and Wright State University (a predominantly white institution approximately 16 miles away in Dayton):

> We have to be able to compete as far as having the same facilities. We don't have a graduate school. We can't fund a graduate school. We just started it back, but the Board of Regents told us they didn't have enough money to fund a graduate school, so they took it away from us. Wright State is down the street. They have a graduate school and get millions of dollars. We're put in a position where we're not supposed to compete.

Tennessee State University

In agreement with Anthony of Central State, both Smith and Porter expressed some of the same concerns regarding integration's impact on the perception of HBCUs. Smith contended that "narrow-minded" people generalize and categorize all African-American organizations, businesses, and educational institutions as inferior. These perceptions have nothing to do with the entities themselves, but rather the fact that they are administered or controlled by African-Americans. Thus, integration would not change these views. Nonetheless, he was optimistic that the strength and character of student bodies and alumni could help these institutions adjust to integration: "I think our history, traditions, culture, and values can be adopted by whoever attends the university. This doesn't mean that other traditions can't be added to this. That's what diversity is about. That's what America ought to be about." Yet, Porter's belief was that integration would compel state governments to give equal funding to HBCUs, but because African-American students would be in the minority, they would not have the opportunity to develop leadership skills and participate in all aspects of college life at the universities, as they do now. Hence, the identity and culture would be destroyed.

Likewise, Tennessee State University respondents also expressed uncertainty about the future control of HBCUs, and whether African Americans would continue to be at the helm of leadership. According to Porter, a lot of the administrators will not be African American. Consequently, the new authorities will bring a different set of values to the decision-making process and will not understand HBCUs' historical significance. Student Government Association President Angela Dixon agreed, saying: "If we integrate and become equal or outnumbered, our voting power and everything that goes on at the university will be diminished. They will have control over everything." Conversely, Smith and Whitfield were a bit more positive. As long as those Caucasians in power mean well, have the university's best interest in mind, and try to help more than to rule, things will work out fine. Whitfield believed that even with integration, African Americans will not have to relinquish all authority, for there will always be competent African Americans in top leadership positions. And last, Qualls-Brooks expressed a more politically correct and diplomatic answer, responding that integration at HBCUs does not threaten African Americans any more than anything else in this country.

Kentucky State University

Regarding the negative external perceptions of HBCUs, Peale, as did Smith of Tennessee State, explained that these are nothing more than stereotypes that were more prevalent before the desegregation and integration processes. In contrast, Coleman said that even though the student body is almost 50 percent Caucasian and other, the local community's mindset still reflects the notion that Kentucky State is inadequate. This is also seen in the negative media attention that Kentucky State sometimes receives, she stated. Furthermore, the Frankfort community supports the University of Kentucky in Lexington (30 miles away) more than Kentucky State: "This isn't to say what the community does do against us, but what they don't do. It's basically an ignoring thing. Maybe the image of the school would change if it was all white, but at 50 percent white, the image still hasn't changed" (Coleman).

Even so, both Peale and Bunton-Douglas do not fear the loss of identity at HBCUs or even the threat of majority-controlled rule. Peale pointed out that Kentucky State University is unique in that, unlike other HBCUs, it has not had a problem in attracting Caucasian students simply because Kentucky State is the only university in Frankfort (the capital of Kentucky), and African Americans make up only 7 percent of Kentucky's 3.5 million people. At the same time, she said that the administration at Kentucky State has remained predominantly African American and this is the way it should be: "I don't mind other people coming in and taking part, but I still think we should be able to decide our own destiny" (Peale). Bunton-Douglas agreed, saying that African-American leaders possess a certain type of sensitivity that others would lack, not because they are racist but simply because they can't understand or relate. However, to supplement this statement, Bunton-Douglas commented that the rich history of these universities can benefit others. "If anything, I think those others will learn some of our history, take some of it, and pass it along."

Alcorn State University

Speaking on integration and whether it will improve the image of HBCUs, Anthony referred to Mississippi's proposal to merge black and white universities (for example, closing Mississippi Valley and merging it with nearby Delta State University). He said this would not be a feasible option, as it would only make matters worse. Payne, however, chose to look at the issue from a stance similar to Bunton-Douglas' of Kentucky State. Integration may improve the image if it enlightens other race people and refutes their preconceived beliefs about HBCUs. To further support his view, he used Alcorn State University's Natchez, Mississippi campus as a concrete example: "Our School of Nursing, which is located in Natchez, is predominantly white and we've been able to attract other race students because we've kept the school on a high level. I think those individuals who are products of the Natchez Center tend to think more positively about the entire university." Also, Payne was optimistic that HBCUs were not in danger of losing their identity. In essence, he was hopeful that one day there will be no need to classify a university as historically white or black and with integration, the "courts will provide the strengths that historically black institutions have always needed, but have never gotten." Anthony did not offer such a utopian viewpoint, for with integration, he envisioned an environment where African-American heritage has been neglected, disregarded, and forgotten. Moreover, African-American administrators may still exist, but they would not have any decision-making power.

Mississippi Valley State University

"No doubt, if integration did occur, our image would probably be enhanced in the white community," Young said. Nevertheless, Baldwin,* like Tennessee State's Smith and Kentucky State's Peale, said that the image is already embedded in others' minds, and the only way it could be altered would be through student, staff, faculty, and alumni efforts, not as a result of integration. She continued, saying that HBCU officials and advocates do want to reach a happy medium, in which HBCUs are desegregated and continue in their role as bastions of African-American history. Young and Walker*, however, were a little more doubtful. Young feared that the gradual loss of African-American leaders in the Southern secondary educational systems during integration and desegregation in the 1960s and 1970s may happen again when implemented in higher education. During this period, many African-American teachers lost their jobs and African-American principals were relegated to lower positions. Walker reiterated a similar view, saying that the curriculum will no longer be geared toward African-American traditions, but will be required to focus on multiculturalistic traditions. Therefore, the identity will be destroyed.

Jackson State University

Throughout her responses, Neal* continued discrediting the idea that HBCUs can not preserve their cultural heritage and diversify simultaneously. Yet, she was also unyielding in her belief that these institutions do not have to be administered by non-blacks in order to be strong and successful. African Americans are capable, competent, and able leaders. The notion that others should control HBCUs is especially apparent when HBCUs encounter financial difficulties, usually the result of inadequate funding. For example, often the "powers that be" incorrectly dub these problems as "mismanagement." In these instances, universities must demonstrate they have used their funding properly. This principle is nothing more than accountability and is applicable to all universities. Perhaps even more important, Neal said that this country revolves around attitudes and perceptions which can not be legislated. Hence, African Americans and HBCU advocates should disregard these perceptions and strive for excellence. Above all, the cultural heritage, traditions, and function of HBCUs can not be diminished: "No matter what a school's enrollment reflects down the line somewhere, you can not erase the fact that these schools were established for the purpose of educating the newly freed. I think people get hung up on semantics sometimes, but the fact remains 'historically black' means just that."

Other Race Objectives at HBCUs and Predominantly White Universities

When asked whether or not HBCUs discriminated, all of the 15 interviewees emphatically responded with a "no," and justified their viewpoints by stating HBCUs have always welcomed diversity, and their doors have always been open. In fact, one commented that HBCUs are more integrated than the predominantly white universities (Porter). And, there are more opportunities for all to excel and advance at HBCUs, including white faculty and staff members who would probably have greater opportunities for more successful careers than their black counterparts at historically white institutions (Payne). This section evaluates if these HBCU representatives subscribed to double standards and inconsistencies when quota systems or other race objectives (certain percentages of minorities) are applied to historically black and historically white institutions. The responses fell along many points on the continuum.

Central State University

Anthony, director of public relations and alumni affairs, said while black institutions should not be expected to implement other race goals and objectives, the predominantly white colleges and universities should institute these same objectives. He provided a few reasons for his opinion. First, he questioned why other race people, or minorities in the case of HBCUs, would consider an HBCU, unless it was because they wanted exposure to a different culture. Second, Central State does not have comparable facilities and resources to Wright State in Dayton: "[At Wright State, they] have access to many things we don't have here. I'm not saying that to put us down, but I am saying that it would be ridiculous to ask us to maintain a quota system for minority students when nobody is providing us the resources to do what we are presently doing." Third, Anthony believed instituting the same kind of standards at predominantly white universities would ensure that they are making a good faith effort to recruit African Americans and others as well. Adding to his argument, Anthony stated that it is easier for historically white institutions to recruit and retain African Americans than it is for HBCUs to recruit and retain Caucasians simply because this is a majority-controlled society in which the perception that African-American institutions are second-class is prevalent. Furthermore, he noted that African Americans have been programmed to accept that white is right, best, and superior.

Tennessee State University

The Tennessee State responses varied widely. Porter (former National Alumni Association President), Whitfield (Alumni Relations Director), and Dixon (Student Government Association President) were all on one accord in saying that neither HBCUs nor historically white institutions should be forced to implement and maintain a quota system, or a certain percentage of minorities. And, if such policies are implemented, they should be equitable and just across the board (Dixon). Moreover, Porter added that he fails to see the necessity of quota systems. In referring to Tennessee State's Stipulation of Settlement, which "requires that we reach some magic percentage [of other race students] in order to have some degree of parity," Porter doubted if that method would ever work. According to Porter, the most simplified resolution to this is to guarantee equal access to all schools and provide support services unique to minority groups so that they are afforded the same opportunities to progress. Even so, Porter did note, as did Central State's Anthony, that recruiting African Americans is much easier for white institutions because they have the money, resources, and that many African Americans think white universities are better.

Both Qualls-Brooks (Director of Public Relations) and Smith (National Alumni Association Vice President) had differing perspectives on quotas. While Qualls-Brooks stated the need for quota systems at HBCUs is contingent on existing conditions, she had more to say about instituting them at predominantly white institutions: "They shouldn't be forced -- they should just do it, like we've [HBCUs] done it. But, if you're not going to do right, then you should be forced. HBCUs have always done right, never turning anybody away." Smith agreed with her, stating that as wrongdoers, predominantly white colleges and universities have "a greater burden to correct that which they have done wrong, and when you're the instigator of segregation, then there should be a greater obligation to do more for [a] longer [period]." This is not to say that all of the responsibility for integrating should be placed on the historically white universities. In order to achieve a white presence on HBCU campuses and to overcome resistance, quotas and goals may be an effective remedy initially. However, these goals should not be permanent solutions (Smith).

Kentucky State University

The answers given by Alumni Affairs Director Peale and Staff Writer Bunton-Douglas reflected Kentucky State University's current integration status. Under a mandate by the Kentucky Council on Public Higher Education, all state-supported institutions must meet specific goals in recruiting other race students and faculty. Ironically, this mandate has had an adverse affect on the amount of African-American faculty at Kentucky State: "I'm in favor of the quota system because that would've forced us to hire more African Americans to teach the kids. The faculty numbers are lagging. Out of 140 faculty, about 30 African Americans are full-time. The desegregation order would put us up to about 42 percent" (Peale). As for maintaining these same other race goals at predominantly white institutions, Bunton-Douglas saw nothing wrong with them because, as Tennessee State's Qualls-Brooks and Smith also said, these institutions "have a history of not letting us in."

In a closely related matter, Peale stated the admission and retention of African Americans at historically white institutions should be looked at separately, as "they are doing great from the admissions standpoint, but on retention they're doing awful." For HBCUs, Peale contended that they are doing a better job at graduating other race students who are admitted. It should also be noted that the Kentucky Council on Public Higher Education has stipulated that none of the state universities can expand programs if they are not in compliance with Kentucky's desegregation plan (Peale).

Alcorn State University

"I'd like to think that eventually we'll get past that. It's unfortunate that we have to force that kind of thing. Sometimes those false things are put in place in an effort to try and make things better," said University Relations Director Payne, in response to quota systems at all institutions. In short, the priority should be providing equal opportunities for all. Nonetheless, he did say that historically white institutions are at an advantage because they have "large, stately buildings," and diverse programs -- "outward trappings" -- that attract African Americans.

Speaking from the student perspective, Acting Student Government Association President Anthony had a different stance on the matter. Reiterating what other HBCU interviewees have said, he felt that minority objectives were not necessary for HBCUs, but were needed at predominantly white schools. In addition, he contradicted Payne's view on recruitment and retention of whites at HBCUs: "Here, we don't isolate ourselves from our colleagues. You can be blue, black, white, pink, or purple, you're still a human being. At Alcorn, it's easier to [recruit] and retain whites because we give them a sense of being -- you're one of us and we like you for that. We're not going to treat you any differently. You got in like I did."

Mississippi Valley State University

At Mississippi Valley State University, the interviewees' responses were quite similar to those responses received from others. To Baldwin,* an alumni relations representative, public education is about choices; therefore, quotas should not be used under any circumstance. The public information coordinator, Young, on the contrary, believed these established goals and objectives are in the best interest of all universities if they want to avoid legal problems. Perhaps the most compelling response was that of Walker,* a Student Government Association member:

> We shouldn't be required to keep a quota system because the schools are historically black universities. But, those [others] who would like to come and who meet the requirements should have the opportunity for an education, but they must realize that this is a school geared toward educating blacks; it is historically black in origin. Harvard and Yale tend to look for their own. Therefore, we must do the same.

And, like many others (Qualls-Brooks, Smith, and Bunton-Douglas), he said that historically white institutions should maintain other race objectives because of their past discriminatory practices. For the most part, the interviewees said it is less difficult for historically white institutions to recruit and retain blacks because of athletics, funding, facilities, and resources (Baldwin; Young; Walker).

Jackson State University

Concluding that her biases would show, Neal,* a public information representative, declined to comment on the use of quotas and other race objectives at HBCUs and historically white universities. She did, however, offer her opinion on whether it is easier for historically white institutions to recruit and retain African Americans than it is for HBCUs to recruit and retain whites. In common with others (D. Anthony, Porter, Payne, and Walker), she said it is easier for white institutions to recruit and retain African Americans, but she gave a different supporting argument. According to Neal, although African Americans have always been more willing to adapt to diverse environments, Caucasians have been a little more reluctant to do the same. Expounding on her point, Neal used a 17 or 18-year-old freshman as her example: "The 17 or 18-year-old white student that HBCUs would be trying to recruit, for the most part, has not lived next door to African Americans, so it's very difficult to adjust to that in a dormitory or on campus." She continued by stating that social functions are an integral part of college life and implied it would be very difficult for a Caucasian student to adjust to the social scene at an HBCU, as it reflects the predominant culture.

The Public Relations Role in Integrating HBCUs

This section examines how HBCUs are coping with the possibility of closure or integration, and the role public relations plays in targeting those publics (alumni and students) who ultimately must deal with these issues. On a surface level, all of the public relations representatives provided unanimous, general responses to those interview questions which sought to find out background information. For instance, no one was certain if anything could be done legally to stop proposed mergers, other than what has been done already -- filing lawsuits and waiting for the courts to decide HBCUs' fate. And, all public relations practitioners responded that they would like to think their respective universities utilize proactive strategies, but in reality, often times the universities must rely on reactive strategies. Finally, four of the public relations staff members said their universities have used a diplomatic and democratic approach in handling dissatisfaction with integration. These methods include: encouraging discussions and dialogue between all involved parties (TSU), working together to "pool resources" (ASU), working with all concerned publics (alumni, students, faculty, and staff) and informing them ahead of time about new developments in the *Ayers* case (MVSU), and using conflict management to resolve differences (JSU) (Qualls-Brooks; Payne; Young; Neal). All 15 participants were asked about their publics' reactions to desegregation and integration, survival strategies that have been implemented, and the role their department plays in executing any survival strategies.

Central State University

Because Central State University has not gone through the integrative process on the same level as the other universities, Anthony was asked about his role within the university. Anthony described himself as the "message carrier" and "traveling salesman" for Central State University. In essence, he tries to promote a positive image of the university and offset those negative forces and occurrences which result in criticism of Central State University. According to Anthony: "I constantly deal with the things we're talking about -- the image of the university, justifying the university, telling the good things about the university, trying to put a positive spin on some of the negative things that happen, and making sure we get our fair share of the good reporting." From his perspective, how he interacts with the public reflects back on the university and how people will perceive Central State University.

Tennessee State University

Just as the answers to the questions have been varied, the reactions from students, faculty, and alumni in response to integration have been diverse as well. Qualls-Brooks diplomatically stated that Tennessee State University has always embraced, accepted, and advocated diversity. In fact, a plus of integration, according to Qualls-Brooks and Smith, is diversity and exposure. "You learn more about others when you realize you live in a world of 'otherness' beyond ourselves and others learn about you. They learn that all of the myths they have known about blacks are not true because they are coming into our house" (Qualls-Brooks). In contrast, other university representatives were more explicit in their descriptions of the various reactions. During his tenure as National Alumni Association President (from 1990 to 1994), Porter said that he witnessed frustration, anger, and hopelessness, especially among the students and alumni. He observed that the students wanted to "maintain a racially identifiable school," meaning a predominantly black student body and administration. Because of these feelings, the students demonstrated on several occasions, Porter said. Similarly, the alumni were upset as well; however, while they wanted to hold on to the image of the university that was a part of their memories, they also recognized the value of integration and "worked toward that." Nevertheless, they too, were adamant about maintaining black leadership in the administration (Porter).

Accordingly, both Whitfield and Dixon expressed the same views, particularly about students:

> A lot of people say that TSU students are prejudiced and don't want white people here. But, what we actually feel is that we don't want to be told what we have to do. Don't make us do anything. We don't mind [white] people being here. Since the beginning, they've been here anyway. Just allow us to continue to be how we are, but don't force us to do anything. (Dixon)

Adding to this, Whitfield commented that many students are very upset by the minority scholarships that are given to some Caucasian students at Tennessee State. Because many African-American students are barely able to handle the financial expenses of college, they feel the scholarships threaten money supplies that could be applied towards their tuition.

Despite resistance to change, survival strategies and plans have been developed to ensure that Tennessee State will continue its legacy as a historically black university. Further, alumni, faculty, and students are all actively involved in the planning (Dixon). The National Alumni Association has helped out with a lot of the legal expenses of *Geier v. Dunn* and has also intervened recently on the Stipulation of Settlement, saying the university has done everything possible to satisfy the requirements and the university wants to be released from the mandate (Porter; Whitfield). Further, throughout the years, Tennessee State University has used integration as a way to improve the institution. For example, under a former administration, the state of Tennessee committed funding for campus renovations. And, currently, the academic program is being upgraded, along with the construction of new buildings like the campus student union center (Porter; Dixon). Moreover, the alumni are also involved in a campaign to raise $100,000 annually for the next three years for scholarship money. This will supplement state funding (Dixon).

And, within the last four or five years, the alumni association has adopted a three-tiered program which emphasizes image-building, fundraising, and recruitment. With recruitment, Whitfield said they have asked the members of the 32 organized alumni chapters to participate by replacing themselves at the university. Nonetheless, Whitfield did admit some of the shortcomings of alumni support, one being the lack of white alumni involvement: "There's no out and out effort to recruit the minority alumni, but no one has come forth. That goes back to a lot of alumni feel that the 'other people' are using us primarily to fulfill their goals. They have not committed to be involved. I have suggested that we do need to reach out a little bit more just to see what we can do." Also, African-American alumni are apathetic as well, as some have become "disenchanted with the desegregation/integration issue and have divorced themselves from the university" (Whitfield).

The Student Government Association has its own strategic agenda as well. According to Dixon, it trains some of Tennessee State's best and brightest students in recruiting strategies and methods. These students are asked to recruit at local predominantly black high schools and at high schools in their hometowns. Dixon saw students as the best resource in keeping their university predominantly African American because "if one person brings back one person, we have doubled our enrollment." In addition, the Student Government Association also works collectively with the alumni, administration, and community in providing tutoring in the African-American community and other service projects as well. Dixon hoped this community service would enhance the image of Tennessee State within the African-American community.

And, as for assistance from external support networks, there has been support from the local

NAACP chapter, a civil rights organization, and the Nashville Ministerial Alliance. However, often times this involvement has been short-lived and would usually occur when there were new developments. Because these groups were not actually in the mainstream of what was going on at the universities, their efforts were somewhat unsuccessful (Whitfield).

Oddly, Qualls-Brooks referred the researcher back to Whitfield for details on survival strategies. But, much to her credit, Porter and Smith supported Qualls-Brooks and the work of her office. Porter commented that for the most part, it would be dangerous for the public relations office to shape and mold the publics' viewpoints on integration, for its purpose is to pass along objective, unbiased information. Likewise, Smith said the public relations office has done an excellent job in using its publications to show the university's diversity.

Kentucky State University

Since Kentucky State University has been integrated with the influx of state government employees during the 1960s, there has been very little overt tension and negative reaction to the integrative process. During the 1970s and 1980s, when Kentucky State was required by the state to meet specific other race goals, it was difficult to get substantial support from organizations such as the NAACP, as NAACP chapters existed mainly in those cities with high African-American populations -- Lexington and Louisville (Peale). Yet, this has not diminished or erased the feelings of those involved with the various aspects of the university. Like Tennessee State University, Kentucky State also has very little participation from its white alumni. And, once integration was implemented full-scale, Peale said there was a rapid and "dramatic" loss of older and black faculty members. Adding to this, Bunton-Douglas said that many African Americans are disillusioned with the integrated campus when they arrive as freshmen, especially since the university is still marketed as an HBCU:

> The students think of an HBCU. They think they're going to come here and that it's going to be all black people and no white people. When they get here, they see there's really a majority of white students. This disturbs them a little bit because they've perceived it as an HBCU; it's a little more of a multicultural student body than what they expected.

Even so, Kentucky State has utilized multifaceted strategies in dealing with the disillusionment, resistance, and adjustment. The Alumni Affairs Office has been actively involved in developing several strategies. First, the National Alumni Association established a legal defense fund to assist with any potential legal battles that may arise about maintaining the university as an HBCU. Second, there are African-American Kentucky State alumni on the Board of Regents, a first in the university's history. Third, in common with Whitfield at Tennessee State, Peale said there has not been an organized effort to recruit the absent white alumni, other than the one-year free membership given to all students upon graduation. Peale explained that many of the white alumni are reluctant to become involved because they don't feel welcomed and often times want to know what they will receive in return for joining. Fortunately, there has been some effort to reach these alumni. According to Peale, she has suggested affinity groups, or offshoots of the Alumni Association. For example, a group of state government employees could have a chapter. Further, Peale is currently sending out surveys to Kentucky alumni (who comprise about one-half of the graduates and many are Caucasian) to assess what they want from the Alumni Association. Last, the president's office hired an outside consulting firm to evaluate the institution and its programs. This internal self-study represented students, faculty, and staff (Peale).

Bunton-Douglas' involvement has been limited to "making the university look good and feeding the media positive information about the programs, what the faculty is doing, and how our students are excelling." She envisioned this as her contribution to the survival of Kentucky State, "the best kept secret in Kentucky." News releases, articles, and the alumni newsletter are used to report university information. Even though Bunton-Douglas uses these methods as a way to disseminate information about Kentucky State, her efforts are somewhat hampered because the university doesn't have a full-time marketing person (Peale; Bunton-Douglas).

Coleman briefly described the role of the Student Government Association as the "students' vehicle and voice." Further, she explained that in recent years, the Student Government Association has not taken any measures regarding the preservation of the university as an HBCU. This is due largely in part because the university is growing and constructing new buildings -- "our campus isn't falling apart." Although Coleman was pleased that Kentucky State isn't suffering financially, she was somewhat skeptical about the sincerity behind campus improvements: "It really makes you wonder. Is it all just for the sake of preserving the university's history, or is it in an effort to say that was the history and this is what we're moving towards now -- a more integrated, culturally diverse university? And, I think that is the push of the university now."

Alcorn State University

Referring to Alcorn's reaction to recent litigation (*U.S. v. Fordice*) and also integration, Anthony had this to say:

> Basically, everyone is handling it in the best way they can because there is no one way to handle this. When [the decision] came out two years ago, there was a lot of hostility because we chose to come to Alcorn for various reasons -- upholding family legacies and tradition. When the *Ayers* case first came to our attention, a lot of my colleagues were very hostile because we weren't bothering anyone.

Contradicting Anthony's stance, Payne simply echoed Tennessee State's Qualls-Brooks by commenting that the Alcorn family has never been opposed to integration, but rather opposed to the potential of being relegated to a subservient role once integration has taken place.

At Alcorn, there have been some survival strategies as well, although not as comprehensive as those at Tennessee State or Kentucky State. According to Anthony, the student body presidents of the eight Mississippi public universities often meet and try to develop feasible and reasonable alternatives to problems resulting from integration demands. All want equal funding and are opposed to any consolidation or mergers. On a campus level, Anthony has kept students informed about recent issues in the *Ayers* case, asked for their input, and encouraged participation in rallies (at the state Capitol), which were organized to preserve the three Mississippi HBCUs.

In a much-related vein, Payne said the university has continued to produce quality students, fundraise to supplement state funding, and strengthen existing programs. More specifically, his office is involved in every aspect of the university. Its function is to enhance the university's image: "If we have a good, strong program and we think it will appeal to all, then public relations has got to get the word out there." Thus, the public relations office has kept students, alumni, and faculty informed about Alcorn's accomplishments in hopes that these publics will think positively about the university (Payne). While speaking on the responsibilities of the public relations office, Payne mentioned one of its weaknesses, which is a lack of community outreach in the areas surrounding Alcorn.

Mississippi Valley State University

As other public relations directors have said, Young reiterated that Mississippi Valley is not opposed to integration. While Baldwin* supported this as well, she also felt that Mississippi Valley needed funding to enhance programs and the physical aspects of the campus. Without these financial resources, it would be very difficult to attract other race people. Her concern was heightened by the March 1995 decision in the *Ayers* case:

> We have been very, very upset over the judge's ruling. The other two historically black institutions received funds. We were told to desegregate and integrate, but were not given anything to do that with. Then we were told to be economically sound by July 1, 1996, but were not given a dime for enhancement. We're elated that we are not closing this year, but we are not satisfied. We will not be satisfied. We're not going to stand by and let them close us. We're going to fight until the very end, even if we have to go back to court to appeal it.

Walker* echoed her concerns, saying that the university is still holding on and will continue to grow and prosper.

Baldwin's and Walker's optimism are reflected in the survival strategies Mississippi Valley has implemented. First, the Alumni Relations office supplies information to the Planning and Implementation Committee, which is comprised of alumni, faculty, and students. In addition, Information Services distributes a brochure that reports updated information on the *Ayers* case, any alumni news, and campus activities (Baldwin). Moreover, Young discussed an economic feasibility study her office distributed to the various publics. This study was devised by the Office of the Vice President for Administration and demonstrated how invaluable Mississippi Valley is in the surrounding community: "We have been trying to impress on the state of Mississippi and the county we are located in that it is very important to their survival that we survive" (Young). The Student Government Association has been instrumental as well by providing motivational and inspirational support and encouragement to the president, administration, and students (Walker). Last, in April 1994, the NAACP, Mississippi Valley, and the other two public Mississippi HBCUs participated in a "March on Jackson," organized by the NAACP. This march, which began at Jackson State and ended at the state Capitol, was an effort to preserve Mississippi's three public black universities (Baldwin).

Jackson State University

Although Neal* maintained that Jackson State University must serve the "broader community" and diversity is a positive end result of integration, she also said the university can not and will not "abandon its heritage." In other words, integration is fine as long as it does not diminish the importance of African-American history. This is how she described the students', faculty's, and alumni's reactions to integration. As for actual survival plans and strategies, Neal did not give any specifics, except to say that all HBCUs must have these plans in tact and be prepared. She did, however, briefly explain that the Public Information Office serves more in a facilitator capacity. That is, it helps prepare university officials who coordinate fundraising activities, athletic events, and develop recruiting strategies: "Everything that goes on is public relations. We work with everybody and try to make sure information and whatever ammunition they need is available." The Alumni Association has participated in rallies as well, and the university is involved in community service activities. In conjunction with the Ford Foundation, Jackson State has established a community development corporation which helps revitalize the surrounding neighborhood. The university sponsors enrichment programs for African-American elementary, middle, and high school students to encourage an interest in the sciences and math.

Public Relations Recruitment and Retention Methods

Building on the role of public relations in integrating HBCUs, this section focuses on public relations efforts that have been used in recruiting and retaining other race students. It should be noted that only the public relations representatives responded in this section.

Central State University

Central State University has not used any particular strategies in recruiting non-blacks or blacks, except publicizing those quality programs which will attract the best and brightest Caucasians and African Americans. As for retaining minority students, Anthony said that Central State faculty, staff, and even the president use "Southern hospitality" and students are encouraged to discuss any problems, no matter what they may entail, with administrative officials. Perhaps Anthony said it best in a *Dayton Daily News* article: "Basically, we were just sort of left alone to do our own thing . . . so we have been pictured as separatist. We're trying to change the way people think about this university. We want to make Central State a personality - - one that is sexless, ageless and colorless" (Haidet 12-Z7).

Tennessee State University

To recruit minority students, Tennessee State has used minority scholarships. This provision is a part of the Stipulation of Settlement mandate. And, the university has employed a method of retention unparalleled at any of the other sample universities -- a Minority Student Affairs Office, which provides counseling and academic assistance to Caucasian students (Qualls-Brooks). When asked if these methods differed for recruiting and retaining African-American students, Qualls-Brooks somewhat shied away from responding. Nonetheless, she said her office addresses this issue in a general manner by telling "the TSU story, no matter who it affects."

Kentucky State University

Perhaps Kentucky State University's Bunton-Douglas offered the most open and candid response. In the university publications that are released from the Public Relations Office, the accomplishments of both black and white students are highlighted. In fact, Bunton-Douglas elaborated on this by sharing her experiences:

> In our publications, we don't discriminate, we show the campus as it is, and it is an integrated campus, whether you like it or not. Just recently, -- and I think it's good public relations to go into the classrooms -- I spent a week just going to classes. I was really shocked. I see the numbers on paper, but when I went to the classrooms, I actually saw how many students are black and white, and how I can better portray the university. I think that gives you a good idea. I really did some adjusting in my strategies. I didn't have to put a black student here or a white student there to pose a shot. It was there happening for me.

Furthermore, Bunton-Douglas stated that she didn't believe the university had any recruitment and retention strategies specific to either black or white students. And, as stated beforehand, unlike other public HBCUs, Kentucky State is in a unique position. The university has not had a problem with attracting Caucasian students, especially since many of them are state government employees or local residents (Bunton-Douglas).

Alcorn State University

At Alcorn State, non-black recruiters have been hired to attract non-black students to the university. These accelerated, specialized recruiting efforts focus on schools with considerable other race numbers. Also, a diversity scholarship program has been implemented. Yet, there have not been many methods used to retain these students, other than academic and social support systems which have been used to retain the traditional clientele of the university (Payne). Payne believed that once there is a white presence on campus, more white students will be apt to come to Alcorn. In common with other universities (Kentucky State), Payne has utilized the public relations publications to emphasize the achievement and successes of Caucasian Alcorn students. Payne hoped that their accomplishments will encourage other Caucasians to come to Alcorn. Although Payne didn't see a difference in those recruitment and retention methods used for Alcorn's African-American students, he did say that perhaps Alcorn could do more.

Mississippi Valley State University

Although Young was not aware of any existing services to recruit and retain minority students in the initial March 1995 interview, strategies have been implemented since then. "An effort is presently being made to hire non-black personnel on faculty and in offices, such as Admissions and Fiscal Affairs, in order to become a more diverse institution. MVSU is [also] actively recruiting faculty and students of non-African-American origin" (Young). In common with Alcorn and Kentucky State, Information Services uses every opportunity to spotlight non-black students in their publications.

Jackson State University

Like Alcorn State, Jackson State's minority recruiters (one of which is a Caucasian Jackson State alumna) target those high schools which have higher concentrations of non-black students. These recruiters serve as mentors for the Caucasian students. Other than this, Neal* said she does not know of any other methods specific to recruiting and retaining a particular group of students.

Summary

The results have revealed not only the passion, sentiment, and frustration revolving around integration demands at HBCUs, but also insightful information about the various survival strategies these six universities have implemented to ensure the future existence of public historically black colleges and universities. Equally important, these responses provided connections to some earlier findings and offered differing perspectives.

Although each university representative responded to the interviews based upon his or her opinion and the position of his or her university in relation to integration, many of the answers were on one accord. First and foremost, HBCUs do serve a multifaceted purpose. These functions include: producing graduates who are able to compete successfully in the world, preserving the deep and rich cultural heritage of people of African and American descent, providing nurturing and social support networks for African Americans, and serving the African-American community and others through political activism and community service. Second, there is a difference between desegregation and integration. While one is more of a legal remedy which seeks to eliminate HBCUs (desegregation), the other (integration) is a moral issue which attempts to provide parity and equality for HBCUs (Porter; Smith). Often times, the concepts are used interchangeably. And, some believe that one may exist in a particular situation while the other does not (Neal). Third, the majority of respondents did fear that it would be difficult for HBCUs to hold onto their cultural traditions while integrating, although it will not be impossible to do both.

Fourth, instituting quotas to achieve integration is a sensitive issue. Whereas some of the respondents did not see the necessity for quotas for any university, others saw more of a need for other race objectives at predominantly white colleges and universities. Fifth, all institutions have implemented some form of public relations strategies to help their publics understand and cope with integration. Last, all universities have also used public relations efforts -- minority scholarships, Minority Student Affairs, minority recruiters, and showing diversity in publications -- to recruit and retain other race students.

Some of the findings were closely linked to prior research. Ironically, much of what Haynes reported years ago is still a factor in the desegregation and integration of public HBCUs. External forces, such as state legislatures and legal suits, continue to be the catalysts for integration. Black college supporters are still concerned about preserving the cultural heritage of HBCUs. Further, many of the administrations at the sample universities remain predominantly African American, and the respondents felt this is the way it should be. Perhaps even more significant, some of the predictions that Haynes' subjects made have come to pass. For example, the most visible impact of desegregation and integration can be observed in the student bodies, as Kentucky State and Tennessee State University prove this. The main goal of HBCUs continues to be the education of African Americans; yet, this is being done while understanding and incorporating diversity (Porter; Walker; Neal). New programs that will attract students from all racial backgrounds are being added to the curriculum, as in Alcorn State's Nursing Program at its Natchez, Mississippi campus. HBCUs like Tennessee State and Jackson State are active in community service. And, the alumni have become more involved in the integration and desegregation processes at their respective universities.

The findings also support Hare, in that HBCUs are not necessarily academically inferior simply because they are predominantly African American. Indeed, HBCUs have produced outstanding and quality graduates. Roebuck and Murty's, and Cunningham's conclusions about diversity can be observed in the student bodies and faculties at the universities. Furthermore, the Student Government Association interviewees from Tennessee State and Kentucky State disclosed some of the same feelings about campus race relations as those student respondents in Roebuck and Murty's study, including the view that white students were competition for an already limited amount of scholarships and financial aid and contact with other race students is very limited outside of class.

Although HBCUs are beginning to move towards progress with integration, much more can be done. Whereas some schools have initiated more comprehensive strategies (Kentucky State and Tennessee State), others seem to be a little less proactive and concerned about integration's impact (Central State). And, the three Mississippi HBCUs are beginning to implement more strategies.

References

Periodical(s)

Haidet, Janice. "CSU Is Concerned with Perceptions." *Dayton Daily News* 8 Dec. 1993: 12-Z7.

Interviews

Anthony, Donald K. Director of Public Relations and Alumni Affairs, Central State University. Personal interview. 1 Feb. 1995.

Anthony, Mark. Student Government Association Acting President, Alcorn State University. Telephone interview. 3 Mar. 1995.

Baldwin, Deirdre. Alumni Relations Representative, Mississippi Valley State University. Telephone interview. 13 Mar. 1995.

Bunton-Douglas, Kimberly. Staff Writer, Kentucky State University. Personal interview. 21 Feb. 1995.

Coleman, Michele. Student Government Association President, Kentucky State University. Personal interview. 21 Feb. 1995.

Dixon, Angela M. Student Government Association President, Tennessee State University. Personal interview. 15 Feb. 1995.

Neal, Rochelle. Public Information Representative, Jackson State University. Telephone interview. 6 Mar. 1995.

Payne, Ralph L. Director of University Relations, Alcorn State University. Telephone interview. 8 Mar. 1995.

_____. Director of University Relations, Alcorn State University. Questionnaire. 7 Oct. 1997.

Peale, Kathy O. Director of Alumni Affairs, Kentucky State University. Personal interview. 21 Feb. 1995.

Porter, Lawrence E. Former National Alumni Association President, Tennessee State University. Personal interview. 31 Jan. 1995.

Qualls-Brooks, Phyllis. Director of Public Relations, Tennessee State University. Personal interview. 16 Feb. 1995.

Smith, Robert L. National Alumni Association Vice President, Tennessee State University. Personal interview. 15 Feb. 1995.

Walker, Marcus. Student Government Association Member, Mississippi Valley State University. Telephone interview. 3 Mar. 1995.

Whitfield, Margaret C. Director of Alumni Relations, Tennessee State University. Personal interview. 16 Feb. 1995.

Young, Wanda R. Information Services Coordinator, Mississippi Valley State University. Telephone interview. 14 Mar. 1995.

_____. Information Services Coordinator, Mississippi Valley State University. Questionnaire. 28 July 1997.

The dedication of black colleges to openness and equal educational opportunity, which is no new development, represents a gamble of the most audacious variety and at the same time is an expression of the belief that they can truly serve *their* [sic.] people and preserve *their* [sic.] culture while they offer an education and a unique experience to people of *all* [sic.] backgrounds.

One theme, however, unites all of them [HBCUs]: attracting, educating, and graduating men and women who otherwise would not have gone to college. The black colleges are aware that, for many of their students, attending college is not a question of *which* [sic.] but of *whether* [sic.]. (Kannerstein 35, 36)

Throughout their existence, all of the HBCUs, especially the public institutions, have endured a great deal whether it was as simple as a name change or as complex as coming to terms with bleak futures. The most recent issue confronting these institutions, integration, has also posed a dilemma for many administrators, faculty, alumni, and students. Finding a compromise between preserving the identity and educational mission of these institutions and diversifying is possible; yet, it will not be an easily attainable goal. Public relations has been instrumental in easing the tension and frustration associated with integration demands, aiding in the transition, and developing survival strategies. Nonetheless, this is only the beginning, for there is always room for improvement. In short, this final chapter will discuss the latest developments in Tennessee's and Mississippi's integration cases, highlight some of the positive features of these institutions and their future challenges, provide some suggestions for supplementing current strategies, and examine the recent changes in the American political and educational systems and what they may imply for historically black colleges and universities.

Recent Developments

As stated beforehand, some Tennessee State University faculty members headed back to court, saying that the university was not progressing toward its other race objective in regards to the student body, which was to be 51 percent other race by the 1995-1996 school year. In 1996-1997, it was approximately 32 percent other race. Therefore, some Tennessee State faculty members (many of whom were professors at UT Nashville before it merged with Tennessee State) proposed a merger between Tennessee State University and Middle Tennessee State University in order to create a racially unidentifiable university. Tennessee State representatives are upset by this, doubting that the merger will come to pass because it appears that neither of the universities has much desire to merge with the other (Smith). Other representatives are doubtful as well, for Whitfield's response was: "No. It's unheard of. The alumni are bitterly opposed to any such mergers taking place." The most compelling and embittered feeling about the merger was expressed by Dixon, the Student Government Association president: "That's just another one of their strategies to get a hold of our heritage and throw it in the trash! We were the only black university that ever merged with a white university [UT Nashville] and came out on top. So, I guess they think if we merge again [with MTSU], they'll [the white university will] come out on top."

This merger has yet to come to pass, and may never become a reality. Even so, Tennessee State, along with its state counterparts, remain under the *Geier* Stipulation of Settlement, also known as the Consent Decree. As recent as March 1997, state officials advocated the termination of the Stipulation of Settlement in light of the Supreme Court's revised standard on determining whether or not a state has adequately desegregated. From their standpoint, Tennessee had satisfied this obligation. A high state court disagreed with this motion, saying that state schools still needed to prove that this is indeed the case ("Recent *Geier* Order," Memo, March 11, 1997). Tennessee State University is but one of several universities still striving for its goal. According to Qualls-Brooks, the following prerequisites must be met by Tennessee State: 51 percent Caucasian full-time undergraduate student enrollment, 51 percent Caucasian faculty, and 50 percent Caucasian administrators.

Other state schools trying to accomplish their other race percentages (increasing black undergraduate enrollment at historically white universities and increasing white undergraduate enrollment at the two historically black universities) include, but are not limited to : UT-Knoxville, Middle Tennessee State University, University of Memphis, and UT-Chattanooga.♦ Only East Tennessee State University and two community colleges had met their other race goals in 1996, which ranged from 3.2 percent to 5.9 percent. Under an extension, all state institutions are to meet their minority goals by the 2000-2001 academic year. These objectives range from 2.8 to 54.2 percent. It is ironic that the goals for the two state HBCUs, Tennessee State and Shelby State Community College, are the highest in the state -- 51 and 54.2 percent, respectively ("Tennessee System" 7).

Likewise, much of the same sentiment of Tennessee State alumni and students has been expressed by some in Mississippi, especially at Mississippi Valley State University, the "university which has always had more to lose than anybody in the *Ayers* case" (Baldwin). On March 7, 1995, Judge Biggers ruled that all eight public universities would remain open. However, while Jackson State and Alcorn State received additional funding, Mississippi Valley did not receive anything. Its future was questioned again after July 1, 1996 (Baldwin).

Mississippi Valley State University supporters received good news in 1996, when the university was spared from a merger with Delta State University. A three-member panel, chosen by the College Board, concluded that it would be detrimental to merge these institutions and that there was a better way to dismantle the dual system of higher education. As a result, the university is well on its way to the road of recovery, as renovations and new constructions are beginning. In addition, the academic programs were enhanced for the 1996-1997 year, with the addition of a new bachelor's chemistry program, a master's degree in criminal justice, and a renewed history program, which had been absent for 10 years (Hawkins, "Merger No Longer" 6; "MS Valley" 46). Despite this progress and jubilation, it looks as if a faction of the *Fordice* plaintiffs (U.S. Justice Department declined inclusion) may continue their pursuit of justice. In late September 1997, they were planning to refile a petition to ask the Supreme Court to review the recent decision and case once more (Healy, "Court Asked" A37). Although the Supreme Court declined a second review of the case, no one knows when this case may draw to a close (Lederman A28). After two decades, however, sooner would probably be less detrimental than later.♦♦

Positive Aspects of HBCUs and Future Challenges

Despite HBCUs' financial crises, inadequate resources and facilities, and uncertain futures (integration, closures, and mergers), the social and educational experiences African-American students receive while attending these institutions should not be disregarded. Roebuck and Murty give several examples of HBCUs' positive features: a less alienated and more comfortable atmosphere for African-American students as opposed to a predominantly white campus, lower drop-out rates, more emotional support, more satisfying social life, more student participation in extracurricular activities, closer student/faculty relationships, and a higher level of psychological comfort because of the presence of African-American traditions and heritage (203).

Even so, these positive features do not diminish the challenges these institutions face, such as increasing library holdings, improving facilities, and addressing white students' feelings of rejection. One of the most pressing challenges is preserving the cultural heritage of these institutions while embracing diversity and integration. For this reason and others as well, it is extremely critical that HBCUs employ additional survival and diversity strategies.

Recommendations for Diversifying

In this time in which America is beginning to understand and accept multiculturalistic traditions and viewpoints, some HBCU critics say these institutions promote separatism, not diversity. In addition, critics say historically black colleges and universities can not continue to justify their position by saying their doors have always been open, and that, unlike other American higher education institutions, they have never denied access to anyone. Indeed, more must be done. Sims has developed some innovative methods that many public HBCUs can implement in order to satisfy integration demands. The following list provides some of these suggestions:

1) Establish a working committee consisting of faculty, staff, students, administrators, minority parents, and community leaders to develop other race recruitment goals (65).

2) Use currently enrolled minority students, staff, and minority alumni in recruiting minority students (66).

3) Recruit at predominantly white churches, secondary schools, and use predominantly white social groups as networks (66).

4) Utilize diversity awareness and training workshops to help everyone understand how to transit from a campus which is geared toward African-American heritage to one which emphasizes multiculturalism (67-68).

5) Hold open house on campuses for minority students and parents. This may help with recruitment and retention (69).

6) If mergers are not feasible, develop consortiums, or cooperative arrangements with nearby predominantly white universities. These benefit all institutions. Types of consortia include: curriculum-centered (sharing academic resources, faculty, programs, etc.), service-centered (sharing library databases or professional development and training in local business

communities), and special purpose (provides opportunity for those faculty and students who are from differing backgrounds to work and research together) (85, 87-89).

7) Advertise events ahead of time in monthly or weekly newsletters in order to encourage minority participation in and support for extracurricular activities (113). Also, if the college/university has a website, this may also be the perfect vehicle to advertise events.

8) Hold extracurricular activities and programs which will appeal to all ethnic groups (114).

9) All individuals involved in all aspects of the university community should demonstrate a commitment to diversity (170).

10) Eliminate and revise any university policies which may tend to encourage and promote discrimination. For example, hiring or promotion practices may seem to favor African Americans (171).

Utilizing public relations tools and strategies as an alternative method to assist in diversifying is crucial as well. Wagener and Smith look at three historically black universities that suffered financially during the 1980s and how their strategic planning enabled them to withstand these fiscal crises. Although the schools -- Fisk University, Tougaloo College, and Howard University -- are private, public institutions can learn from and incorporate some of these strategies as needed. Including everyone from administration to students in the planning process, and building on those positive aspects and assets which have made the college what it is, is absolutely essential (49).

Whiting agrees, saying that integration while simultaneously maintaining HBCUs' historic and educational roles is not impossible. However, administrators must be willing to develop and implement five and ten-year survival plans that will cut costs and eliminate duplicative programs. In addition, creating new curriculae which will appeal to all students, regardless of age, race or ethnicity, will be in the institutions' best interest. Above all, integration is necessary for the continued growth and existence of black colleges: "Only when it is more widely perceived by the leaders of black institutions that survival involves planning for new and broader missions in an unsheltered, integrated, highly competitive environment will they arrive at an antidote for predictable, progressive oblivion" (11).

Providing a differing approach, Culbertson suggests a few strategies that all public relations practitioners should incorporate when dealing with various publics. In essence, public relations staff must be sensitive to their publics' (administration, alumni, faculty, staff, and students) needs and viewpoints, bearing in mind the long and short-term consequences of their decisions. That is, how public relations people define meaning or assess a situation may be completely different from the way others will assess the same situation. Respecting each others' views is the key ("Role Taking" 37, 39, 41-42). Without mutual respect, disagreements will be inevitable and will therefore weaken the institution's infrastructure and any attempts to integrate and diversify. And, the various roles that public relations managers play can have a lasting impact on a college's integration efforts. These roles are:

• The *Expert Prescriber* tries to define and solve problems without regard to the client or publics involved.

- The *Communication Facilitator*, or "mediator/liaison," attempts to make sure all sides of an issue are expressed.
- The *Problem-Solving Process Facilitators*' main goal is proactive planning and ensuring that problems are clearly defined and long-term goals are developed ("Role Taking" 54).

Certainly, breadth of perspective, or an awareness of and appreciation for viewpoints differing from one's own, is a concept that is applicable to the various publics at HBCUs and their feelings about diversity and integration. Culbertson believes that this philosophy supports a free marketplace of ideas, encourages the merging of unique perspectives, and promotes the two-way symmetric public relations model in which all sides of an issue are discussed ("Breadth of Perspective" 18, 21). Indeed, the public relations respondents at the universities included in this work can be described as both communication facilitators and problem-solving process facilitators. By coupling some of these suggestions with those strategies already in place, public historically black colleges and universities will be moving closer to achieving diversity.

Implications

There have been many current events in the American political and higher educational system that may have a profound influence on historically black colleges and universities. HBCU administrators can not afford to ignore the backlash against affirmative action, and the threat to minority scholarships. All of these may have an impact on HBCUs' continued existence and their integration efforts either for the better -- or the worse.

Affirmative action, a governmental program whose purpose is to ensure equal opportunities and access for qualified minorities and women in the workplace and in education, may soon be a practice of the past. At one point, the Republican-controlled Congress' agenda included eliminating affirmative action in hopes of balancing the federal budget and deficit (Massaquoi 72). Many states have been inclined to follow suit as well.

Both Texas and California are in the spotlight, as the nation watches their state legislatures, voters, and U.S. Circuit Courts of Appeals implement policies which threaten not only the American higher educational system, but equal access as well.♦♦♦ The controversial *Hopwood v. The State of Texas*, concluded that the University of Texas Law School at Austin must utilize race-neutral admissions policies. And, state lawmakers are pushing that all state schools adopt and put in place race-neutral policies in hiring and admissions. Similarly, California voters passed the Proposition 209 Initiative in the fall of 1996. This proposal serves to eliminate all affirmative action programs in public higher education facilities. This will apply to hiring, admissions, promotions and contracting decisions. The major sponsor of Proposition 209, Ward Connerly, plans to propose similar legislation to the U.S. Congress. In both cases, the Ninth Circuit Court of Appeals (California) and the Fifth Circuit Court of Appeals (Texas and also instrumental in *Fordice*) ruled that these decisions do not violate the U.S. Constitution (Fields 28, 29). Without affirmative action, more African Americans may choose historically black institutions over predominantly white universities simply because they will have easier access to HBCUs. Indeed, one need look no further than public higher education systems in Texas and California, which have reportedly experienced severe declines in minority enrollment and admissions in the years since these initiatives have been implemented. Thus, HBCUs may be needed now more than ever.

Similarly, a federal appeals court ruled in November 1994 that the Benjamin Banneker

Scholarship, a merit-based scholarship given to African-American students at the University of Maryland at College Park, was unconstitutional because it discriminated against Caucasians and other ethnic groups. If this case sets a precedent, other similar scholarship programs may be abolished as well (Jones 128).

This could have one or two outcomes for historically black institutions. As with the loss of affirmative action, there may be an influx of African Americans choosing to attend HBCUs. After all, minority scholarships will not be an option at the predominantly white universities, thereby decreasing African Americans' chances of attending many of these institutions. On the other hand, this may have an impact on those HBCUs like Tennessee State University, which utilize minority scholarships as an initiative to encourage other race students to enroll at the university. In short, if the majority institutions do away with affirmative action policies, it would stand to reason that HBCU institutions will have to do likewise. What effect will this have on integration efforts? HBCUs may lose some students or may be forced to develop other methods to attract other race students.

Alabama State University has witnessed firsthand the two-edged sword of race-based scholarships. An Alabama State African-American graduate student sued the university because he was denied a scholarship application that is for Caucasian students only. As with other states, a judge developed these scholarships as a method to aid in higher education desegregation in the state's HBCUs ("Ways & Means" A42).

Last, student loans and grants are constantly in grave danger of being cut. In 1994, Congress proposed that the amount of interest on loans should accumulate while students are still enrolled in school. This is contradictory to one of loans' advantages, as the common practice is to defer interest until the student graduates or is no longer enrolled in school. The enforcement of this plan would have caused "student loans [to] jump by 20 to 30 percent" (Manegold A26). This, too, would adversely impact HBCUs, as many African-American students who attend these universities rely on some form of financial aid. If enrollment drops significantly, these institutions will have a difficult time surviving financially.

Fortunately, educational spending has become a top priority, as federal Congressional leaders, once again, grappled with student financial assistance and HBCU funding in their 1998 budget. Often, the White House, House, and Senate proposals provided for different funding levels, making it more difficult to find common ground and achieve a compromise. Nevertheless, Congress finally reached a consensus on 1998 funding legislation. HBCU undergraduate institutions received $118.5 million, while their graduate counterparts received $25 million.♦♦♦♦ This increased from the 1997 funding which was $108.9 million and $19.6 million, respectively. And, $614 million went towards the SEOG (Federal Supplemental Education Opportunity Grants) program, increasing from $583.4 million in 1997. Further, the White House, House, and Senate plans agreed on the Pell Grant maximum at $3,000. In 1997, the average student was only eligible for $2,700. College work study programs remained consistent at $830 million, while Perkins Loans dropped to $165 million (Dervarics "Senate Clears" 6). Hopefully, the increase in money allocated to the aforementioned educational initiatives will continue to assist HBCUs and their students.

Perhaps just as important to all students -- especially African-American students, President Clinton and Congress agreed on and passed a new tax plan to benefit middle- and low- income college students and their parents/guardians. Some of these provisions include a tax credit for qualified families and students on the first $1,000 of college tuition and 50 percent on the next $1,000 of tuition, totaling $1,500; tax deductions for students on a maximum of $2,500 annually on paid student loan interest, and "penalty-free IRA (Individual Retirement Accounts) withdrawals," in which the funds are applied toward college expenses (Dervarics, "Congress Passes" 8).

External HBCU Advocacy Organizations and the Future of HBCUs

One of the most pressing and crucial issues facing public historically black colleges and universities is integration. How HBCU administrators handle this matter could either guarantee the continued existence of these institutions into the next century as beacons for many African Americans and others as well, or destroy an integral part of African-American heritage. Surely, this issue is not going to fall along the wayside anytime soon, as current litigation which has lasted two to three decades in Mississippi and Tennessee, demonstrates. The solution at this time seems to point to public relations survival strategies and plans. Many HBCUs have these strategies in place, but only time will tell how successful they will be.

If public relations strategies prove to be ineffective, the result may be the eradication of HBCUs. While the survival of these institutions remains uncertain, HBCU advocates remain optimistic. The key is to balance and preserve the African-American culture indigenous to HBCUs and embrace multiculturalism wholeheartedly. According to James A. Hefner, Tennessee State University's president: "My responsibility is to make sure we understand from whence we came, but within the midst of diversity" (Mercer, "The Ambiguous" A32).

Furthermore and just as important, it is critical that all HBCU proponents and advocates remain vigilant, as it is dangerous to become content with the "status quo." Believing that black colleges and universities are entitled to such federal funds as Title III-B, can be detrimental. *Hopwood* and Proposition 209 are perhaps foreshadowing what may become the norm in the near future. And, it is absolutely imperative that African Americans take note and realize that hope can no longer be placed solely within the American government. It is important to remember that most legislators are not concerned about the continued existence of historically black colleges and universities. That is, only 19 states, Washington D.C., and one territory are homes to these vital treasures. Many of these states, like Louisiana, Alabama, Missouri, and North Carolina, have endured political and legal battles revolving around desegregation and eliminating dual systems of higher education. The survival of these institutions have virtually no impact on the majority of Congressional leaders' constituents. As such, financial support could cease at any moment.

During the 1997 National Historically Black Colleges and Universities Week (September 21 through September 27), President Clinton declared:

> Historically Black Colleges and Universities have done more to make the American Dream a reality for African Americans than has any other set of institutions in our country. . . .We can continue to count on them to make vital contributions to our Nation's success and to ensure that America lives up to our fundamental values of equality and opportunity. (The White House Office of the Press Secretary Press Release)

While it is impressive and crucial that the President pledges his unwavering support for these educational institutions, HBCU advocates must and can lend their assistance by endorsing and utilizing those external supporting agencies, organizations and resources which serve as a voice for all HBCUs and testify to their academic excellence. They include the following:

- **The White House Initiative on Historically Black Colleges and Universities:** In short, this organization's primary purpose is to serve as a liaison between HBCUs and the federal government and the private sector. Since 1980, it has ensured that HBCUs are remembered in policy-making, positioned HBCUs to receive funding from the public and private sectors, and exposed HBCUs' teaching and learning philosophies to the nation (*White House Initiative* 5).

- **National Association for Equal Opportunity in Higher Education (NAFEO):** This consortium of all HBCUs as well as the predominantly black institutions, has been a beacon of hope and trailblazer for black colleges and universities since 1969. Its main focus is developing programs, policies, and strategies which will strengthen its member institutions and increase the number of African Americans enrolling in HBCUs. Annually, NAFEO hosts regional, state, and national conferences and symposiums (*Keeping the Doors of Opportunity Open*, 1997 NAFEO Conference Program booklet).

- **The College Fund/United Negro College Fund (UNCF):** Whereas NAFEO is inclusive of all HBCUs, UNCF only supports the 41 private HBCUs. Because these universities lack the state funding that their sister, public institutions receive, a vehicle was needed to supplement alumni's and philanthropist's gifts and contributions. UNCF is well-renowned for its fundraising events, the most famous being the annual, televised Lou Rawls "Parade of Stars" telethon. The College Fund/UNCF was established in 1944 (The President's Board of Advisors on Historically Black Colleges and Universities 19).

- **Honda Campus All-Star Challenge:** Sponsored by American Honda Motor Company, each spring HBCU teams are invited to participate in a scholastic "Jeopardy-like" competition. The national champion institution receives a $50,000 grant (*Honda Campus All-Star Challenge: Meeting of the Minds* brochure).

- **Nissan HBCU Summer Institute:** This program is for HBCU faculty. It enhances their skills and knowledge, exposes them to cutting-edge technology, and arms them with new and innovative methods to teach their students ("Nissan HBCU Summer Institute" radio commercial).

- **1996-1997 Guide to Historically Black Colleges and Universities:** A collaborative effort between the Central Office of the Chevrolet Motor Division and *Ebony* magazine, this guide provides brief histories on all HBCUs, as well as addresses, phone numbers, and names of Admissions Officers. In addition, it lists scholarships available for African Americans, and gives brief tidbits on completing financial aid forms, admissions applications, and preparing for college (1996-1997 Guide to Historically Black Colleges and Universities). It is an excellent tool for disseminating information about HBCUs and is published annually.

Final Thoughts and Reflections

Imagine walking in the same footsteps as Martin Luther King, Jr., John Hope Franklin, Nikki Giovanni, W.E.B. DuBois, Marian Wright Edelman, Douglas Wilder, and Oprah Winfrey. Each day, thousands of African-American students do follow these footsteps on the campuses of black colleges and universities, the alma maters of these African-American political, historical, literary, and entertainment figures. It does something for the soul to know that you are in the midst of African-American history -- her past, present, and future. HBCUs do more than just cultivate the mind. They cultivate nurturing, familial, eternal relationships with faculty, staff, and fellow students. And, they provide an environment in which young African-American adults are exposed to other African-American peers who are striving for academic excellence.

This awesome power, energy, and synergy is rarely observed and experienced at the historically white institutions or in the communities these young academicians lived in prior to attending colleges. What a travesty to let these invaluable treasures die a cold, long, and virtually unnoticed death! HBCUs and churches are the only foundations left in the African-American community that are owned, administered, and governed by African-Americans. Once they are eliminated, they can never be regained. This is the cry of many black college advocates.

This is neither an argument in favor of keeping historically black institutions all black nor an attempt to belittle the white institutions, but rather a plea to encourage the preservation of these entities through sharing with others their importance and significance, and explaining that they do not reject multiculturalism and diversity. However, they do and must continue to serve their number one clients, African-American students, first and foremost. If they do not, who will? The present political climate proves this. Having exposure to both worlds, I can truly say that the "HBCU Experience" was one of a lifetime, preparing me for the real world and my graduate schooling at a majority institution. Academically and psychologically, I was a survivor, fighter, and winner. Where would many alumni be without these educational bastions? Where would I be?

Indeed, everyone -- African Americans, Caucasians, Asians, Hispanics -- must realize that there is much sentiment, passion, and sincerity revolving around the preservation and importance of historically black colleges and universities and integration. Further, it must be understood that it is inconsistent to require HBCUs to endorse and embrace full-scale integration, when historically white institutions are not forced to make the same drastic, sweeping changes in their student bodies, faculties, administrations, and staff. They have never been asked to reach a 50/50 goal and will never be asked to do so.

However, it is equally important to understand that African Americans are not faultless either and must bear most of the responsibility in supporting HBCUs, their heritage, and legacies. It is imperative that the African-American community be proactive, not reactive. Often, there is a complacent and standoffish attitude about these colleges, thereby resulting in a severe lack of support, abandonment, and neglect. Maybe this is because little is known about HBCUs or no one cares to know what is transpiring or provide assistance until it is too late. Perhaps the prevailing thought is that these higher learning institutions are inferior and were good enough only for our African ancestors. Regardless of what the reasoning or logic may be, it is critical that African Americans equip themselves with political and legal knowledge to stay abreast on those issues which threaten historically black colleges and universities.

There is much work to be done, and African American organizations are charged with the task of disbursing information and utilizing other initiatives to save these educational institutions. It is imperative that the community write Congressional leaders, especially the Black Congressional Caucus, and ask them to support black colleges. Also, contacting some of the aforementioned black college advocacy organizations and lending support, no matter how great or small, is critical. Encourage high school students to go on black college tours. And, if you are fortunate enough to live in a city or region that sponsors the annual, classic football games (Indianapolis' Circle City Classic, Columbus' Capital City Classic, St. Louis' Gateway Classic, San Diego's Gold Coast Classic, and New Orleans' Bayou Classic, to name a few) featuring black college teams, attend them. These events provide exposure to HBCUs and are scholarship fundraisers. Finally, the nine African-American fraternal organizations (the majority of which were established at HBCUs), the African-American religious denominations, and black college alumni associations can develop collaborative efforts and strategies, and build support networks to further the HBCU cause. The late Benjamin E. Mays, a former Morehouse College (a private HBCU in Atlanta) president from 1940-1967, said it most prophetically:

> If America allows black colleges to die, it will be the worst kind of discrimination and denigration known in history. To decree that colleges born to serve Negroes are not worthy of surviving now that white colleges accept Negroes would be a damnable act.
>
> No one has ever said that Catholic colleges should be abolished because they are Catholic. Nobody says that Brandeis and Albert Einstein must die because they are Jewish. Nobody says that Lutheran and Episcopalian schools should go because they are Lutheran or Episcopalian. Why should Howard University be abolished because it is known as a black university? Why pick out Negro colleges and say they must die? Blot out these colleges: You blot out the image of black men and women in education. . . Integration must never mean the liquidation of black colleges. Every good college and every college that is needed has a right to live. (27)

At Press Time:

♦Finally, the first university in the University of Tennessee System, UT-Chattanooga, reached its court-mandated minority undergraduate percentage during the 1998-1999 academic year. Approximately 16.2% of its 7,323 undergraduates are minorities ("UTC Surpasses" 10).

♦♦HBCU advocates received confirmation of black colleges' value with the release of a recent report entitled *Further Desegregation of Higher Education in the Mississippi Delta*. One of the most compelling recommendations in this report, once more, was to increase the state funding allotted to these universities. The proposal also suggested the establishment of an engineering program at Jackson State, reasoning that these efforts would enhance the racial diversity at the historically black colleges. The aforementioned matters will be addressed by the state legislature sometime in 1999 (Boulard 16, 17).

♦♦♦In the November 1998 election, the voters of Washington passed Initiative 200, a proposal very similar to California's Proposition 209 (St. John 12). Time will tell if the end results will be the same.

♦♦♦♦The 1999 Congressional budget bill approved $134.5 million and $30 million for undergraduate HBCUs and graduate HBCUs, respectively (Dervarics, "HBCU, HSI" 8).

References

Books

Culbertson, Hugh M. "Breadth of Perspective: An Important Concept for Public Relations." *Public Relations Research Annual.* Eds. Larissa A. Grunig and James E. Grunig. Vol. 1. Hillsdale, NJ: Lawrence Erlbaum Associates, 1989. 3-25.

_____. "Role Taking and Sensitivity: Keys to Playing and Making Public Relations Roles." *Public Relations Research Annual.* Eds. Larissa A. Grunig and James E. Grunig. Vol. 3. Hillsdale, NJ: Lawrence Erlbaum Associates, 1991. 37-65.

Kannerstein, Gregory. "Black Colleges: Self-Concept." *Black Colleges in America: Challenge, Development, Survival.* Eds. Charles V. Willie and Ronald R. Edmonds. New York: Teachers College Press, 1978. 29-50.

Mays, Benjamin E. "The Black College in Higher Education." *Black Colleges in America: Challenge, Development, Survival.* Eds. Charles V. Willie and Ronald R. Edmonds. New York: Teachers College Press, 1978. 19-28.

Roebuck, Julian B., and Komanduri S. Murty. *Historically Black Colleges and Universities: Their Place in American Higher Education.* Westport, CT: Praeger Publishers, 1993.

Sims, Serbrenia J. *Diversifying Historically Black Colleges and Universities: A New Higher Education Paradigm.* Westport, CT: Greenwood Press, 1994.

Periodicals

Boulard, Garry. "New *Fordice* Report May Benefit Mississippi HBCUs." *Black Issues In Higher Education* 6 Aug. 1998: 16-17.

Dervarics, Charles. "Congress Passes Tax, Budget Plan." *Black Issues In Higher Education* 21 Aug. 1997: 8.

_____. "HBCU, HSI Funds Clear Congress." *Black Issues In Higher Education* 12 Nov. 1998: 8.

_____. "Senate Clears Student Aid, HBCU Funding Bill." *Black Issues In Higher Education* 27 Nov. 1997: 6.

Fields, Cheryl D. "Surveying the Battleground in the Fight for Access." *Black Issues In Higher Education* 15 May 1997: 28-29.

Hawkins, B. Denise. "Merger No Longer a Threat For Mississippi Valley State." *Black Issues*

In Higher Education 13 June 1996: 6-7.

Healy, Patrick. "Court Asked to Review Mississippi Desegregation Case." *The Chronicle of Higher Education* 26 Sept. 1997: A37.

Jones, Elaine R. "Higher Learning." *Essence* Apr. 1995: 128.

Lederman, Douglas. "High Court Bars Review of Mississippi Case." *The Chronicle of Higher Education* 30 Jan. 1998: A28.

"MS Valley to Offer New Academic Programs." *Black Issues In Higher Education* 11 July 1996: 46.

Manegold, Catherine S. "New Majority's Agenda: Substantial Changes May Be Ahead (Education)." *The New York Times* 11 Nov. 1994: A26.

Massaquoi, Hans J. "What the Republican Sweep of Congress Means to Blacks." *Ebony* Feb. 1995: 68+.

Mercer, Joye. "The Ambiguous Success of Desegregation at Tennessee State U." *The Chronicle of Higher Education* 5 May 1993: A32-A33.

St. John, Eric. "Taking the Initiative: In the Wake of Washington State's Passage of Initiative 200, Pro-Affirmative Action Scholars Call for a New Combat Strategy." *Black Issues In Higher Education* 26 Nov. 1998: 12-15.

"Tennessee System Fails Diversity Test." *Black Issues In Higher Education* 29 May 1997: 7.

"UTC Surpasses Undergraduate Desegregation Target." *Black Issues In Higher Education* 10 Dec. 1998: 10.

Wagener, Ursula, and Edgar E. Smith. "Maintaining a Competitive Edge: Strategic Planning for Historically Black Institutions." *Change* Jan.-Feb. 1993: 40-49.

"Ways & Means." *The Chronicle of Higher Education* 5 Sept. 1997: A42.

Whiting, Albert N. "Black Colleges: An Alternative for Survival." *Change* Mar.-Apr. 1988: 10-11.

Interviews

Baldwin, Deirdre. Alumni Relations Representative, Mississippi Valley State University. Telephone interview. 13 Mar. 1995.

Dixon, Angela M. Student Government Association President, Tennessee State University. Personal interview. 15 Feb. 1995.

Qualls-Brooks, Phyllis. Director of Public Relations, Tennessee State University. Questionnaire. 20 Aug. 1997.

Smith, Robert L. National Alumni Association Vice President, Tennessee State University. Personal interview. 15 Feb. 1995.

Whitfield, Margaret C. Director of Alumni Relations, Tennessee State University. Personal interview. 16 Feb. 1995.

Miscellaneous

American Honda Motor Corporation. *Honda Campus All-Star Challenge: Meeting of the Minds.* Brochure. Sherman Oaks, CA: 1992.

1996-1997 Guide to Historically Black Colleges and Universities. Chicago: Johnson Publishing Company, 1996.

National Association for Equal Opportunity in Higher Education. *Keeping the Doors of Opportunity Open.* NAFEO Conference Program Booklet, 22nd National Conference on Blacks in Higher Education. Washington: 1997.

Nissan Motor Corporation, U.S.A. "Nissan HBCU Summer Institute." Commercial. Gospel 1600/KATZ, St. Louis. 2 Oct. 1997.

The President's Board of Advisors on Historically Black Colleges and Universities. *A Century of Success: Historically Black Colleges and Universities, America's National Treasure.* 1995-1996 Annual Report. Washington: Sept. 1996.

President William (Bill) J. Clinton. "Proclamation on National Historically Black Colleges and Universities Week, 1997." Press Release. New York: Office of the Press Secretary, 22 Sept. 1997.

"Recent *Geier* Order." Memo, Tennessee Board of Regents. 11 Mar. 1997.

White House Initiative on Historically Black Colleges and Universities. Pamphlet. Washington: GPO.

(1) Alabama A&M University, 1875 (Normal, Alabama)

(2) Alabama State University, 1874 (Montgomery, Alabama)

(3) Albany State College, 1903 (Albany, Georgia)

(4) Alcorn State University, 1871 (Lorman, Mississippi)

(5) Allen University,* 1870 (Columbia, South Carolina)

(6) Arkansas Baptist College,* 1884 (Little Rock, Arkansas)

(7) Barber-Scotia College,* 1867 (Concord, North Carolina)

(8) Benedict College,* 1870 (Columbia, South Carolina)

(9) Bennett College,* 1873   (Greensboro, North Carolina)

(10) Bethune-Cookman College,* 1904 (Daytona Beach, Florida)

(11) Bluefield State College, 1895 (Bluefield, West Virginia)

(12) Bowie State University, 1865 (Bowie, Maryland)

(13) Central State University, 1887 (Wilberforce, Ohio)

(14) Cheyney University, 1837 (Cheyney, Pennsylvania)

(15) Claflin College,* 1869 (Orangeburg, South Carolina)

(16) Clark-Atlanta University,* 1869-Clark College; 1865-Atlanta University; 1989-Merger
    resulting in Clark-Atlanta (Atlanta, Georgia)

(17) Coppin State College, 1900 (Baltimore, Maryland)

(18) Delaware State University, 1891 (Dover, Delaware)

(19) Dillard University,* 1869 (New Orleans, Louisiana)

(20) Edward Waters College,* 1866 (Jacksonville, Florida)

(21) Elizabeth City State University, 1891 (Elizabeth City, North Carolina)

(22) Fayetteville State University, 1877 (Fayetteville, North Carolina)

(23) Fisk University,* 1866 (Nashville, Tennessee)

(24) Florida A&M University, 1877 (Tallahassee, Florida)

(25) Florida Memorial College,* 1879 (Miami, Florida)

(26) Fort Valley State College, 1895 (Fort Valley, Georgia)

(27) Grambling State University, 1901 (Grambling, Louisiana)

(28) Hampton University,* 1868 (Hampton, Virginia)

(29) Harris-Stowe State College, 1857 (St. Louis, Missouri)

(30) Howard University,* 1867 (Washington, D.C.)

(31) Huston-Tillotson College,* 1876 (Austin, Texas)

(32) Interdenominational Theological Center,* 1958 (Atlanta, Georgia)

(33) Jackson State University, 1877 (Jackson, Mississippi)

(34) Jarvis Christian College,* 1912 (Hawkins, Texas)

(35) Johnson C. Smith University,* 1867 (Charlotte, North Carolina)

(36) Kentucky State University, 1886 (Frankfort, Kentucky)

(37) Knoxville College,* 1875 (Knoxville, Tennessee)

(38) Lane College,* 1882 (Jackson, Tennessee)

(39) Langston University, 1897 (Langston, Oklahoma)

(40) LeMoyne-Owen College,* 1862 (Memphis, Tennessee)

(41) Lincoln University, 1866 (Jefferson City, Missouri)

(42) Lincoln University, 1854 (Lincoln University, Pennsylvania)

(43) Livingstone College,* 1879 (Salisbury, North Carolina)

(44) Meharry Medical College,* 1876 (Nashville, Tennessee)

(45) Miles College,* 1905 (Birmingham, Alabama)

(46) Mississippi Valley State University, 1946 (Itta Bena, Mississippi)

(47) Morehouse College,* 1867 (Atlanta, Georgia)

(48) Morgan State University, 1867 (Baltimore, Maryland)

(49) Morris Brown College,* 1881 (Atlanta, Georgia)

(50) Morris College,* 1908 (Sumter, South Carolina)

(51) Norfolk State University, 1935 (Norfolk, Virginia)

(52) North Carolina A&T University, 1891 (Greensboro, North Carolina)

(53) North Carolina Central University, 1910 (Durham, North Carolina)

(54) Oakwood College,* 1896 (Huntsville, Alabama)

(55) Paine College,* 1882 (Augusta, Georgia)

(56) Paul Quinn College,* 1872 (Waco, Texas)

(57) Philander-Smith College,* 1877 (Little Rock, Arkansas)

(58) Prairie View A&M University, 1876 (Prairie View, Texas)

(59) Rust College,* 1866 (Holly Springs, Mississippi)

(60) St. Augustine's College,* 1867 (Raleigh, North Carolina)

(61) Saint Paul's College,* 1888 (Lawrenceville, Virginia)

(62) Savannah State College, 1890 (Savannah, Georgia)

(63) Shaw University,* 1865 (Raleigh, North Carolina)

(64) South Carolina State University, 1896 (Orangeburg, South Carolina)

(65) Southern University, Baton Rouge, 1880 (Baton Rouge, Louisiana)

(66) Southern University, New Orleans, 1959 (New Orleans, Louisiana)

(67) Southern University, Shreveport, 1964 (Shreveport, Louisiana)

(68) Spelman College,* 1881 (Atlanta, Georgia)

(69) Stillman College,* 1876 (Tuscaloosa, Alabama)

(70) Talladega College,* 1867 (Talladega, Alabama)

(71) Tennessee State University, 1912 (Nashville, Tennessee)

(72) Texas College,* 1894 (Tyler, Texas)

(73) Texas Southern University, 1947 (Houston, Texas)

(74) Tougaloo College,* 1869 (Tougaloo, Mississippi)

(75) Tuskegee University,* 1881 (Tuskegee, Alabama)

(76) University of Arkansas, Pine Bluff, 1873 (Pine Bluff, Arkansas)

(77) University of District of Columbia, 1851 (Washington, D.C.)

(78) University of Maryland, Eastern Shore, 1886 (Princess Anne, Maryland)

(79) University of the Virgin Islands, 1962 (Saint Thomas, Virgin Islands)

(80) Virginia State University, 1882 (Petersburg, Virginia)

(81) Virginia Union University,* 1865 (Richmond, Virginia)

(82) Voorhees College,* 1897 (Denmark, South Carolina)

(83) West Virginia State College, 1891 (Institute, West Virginia)

(84) Wilberforce University,* 1856 (Wilberforce, Ohio)

(85) Wiley College,* 1873 (Marshall, Texas)

(86) Winston-Salem State University, 1862 (Winston-Salem, North Carolina)

(87) Xavier University,* 1915 (New Orleans, Louisiana)

Sources: *The African-American Almanac* **751- 757; Roebuck and Murty 98-101; The President's Board of Advisors on Historically Black Colleges and Universities 1-15 (Appendix B).**

It should be noted that the remaining HBCUs that would account for the 109 HBCUs are junior or community colleges. Because they do not receive national visibility and are usually attended by local residents, they were not included in this list.

*Denotes the private institutions.

- Debbie Allen (1950-), actress, dancer, choreographer, producer; Howard University, 1971.

- Thomas Jefferson Byrd (c. 1952-); actor; Morris Brown College, 1973.

- Marva Collins (1936-), educator; Clark [Atlanta] University, 1957.

- Spencer Christian (1947-), former *Good Morning America* weather forecaster; Hampton University, 1970.

- Ossie Davis (1917-), actor; Howard University, 1939.

- David Dinkins (1927-), former New York mayor; Howard University, 1950.

- W.E.B. DuBois (1868-1963), educator, sociologist, writer; Fisk University, 1888.

- Billy Eckstine (1914-1993), musician; attended Howard University for one year.

- Marian Wright Edelman (1939-), founder of Children's Defense Fund; Spelman College, 1960.

- Ralph Ellison (1914-), writer; attended Tuskegee University from 1933-1936.

- Medgar Evers (1925-1963), Civil Rights Activist; Alcorn State University, 1952.

- James Farmer (1920-1999), founder of Congress of Racial Equality (CORE); Wiley College, 1938 and Howard University, 1941.

- Roberta Flack (1939-), singer; Howard University, 1958.

- John Hope Franklin (1915-), historian, writer, Chairman of President Clinton's Initiative on Race; Fisk University, 1935.

- Willie E. Gary (1947-), nationally renown personal injury attorney; Shaw University, 1971 and North Carolina Central Law School, 1974.

- Nikki Giovanni (1943-), poet; Fisk University, 1967.

- Alex Haley (1921-1992), author of *Roots* and *Queen*; attended Elizabeth City State University from 1937-1939.

- Alcee L. Hastings (1936-), Congressional Black Caucus Vice Chairman, 103rd Congress; Fisk University, 1958 and Florida A&M University, 1963.

- Benjamin Hooks (1925-), former NAACP national leader; attended LeMoyne-Owen from 1941-1943 and attended Howard University from 1943-1944.

- Reverend Jesse Jackson (1941-), Civil Rights Activist and former presidential candidate; North Carolina A&T University, 1964.

- Maynard Jackson (1938-), former Atlanta mayor; Morehouse College, 1956 and North Carolina Central Law School, 1959.

- Samuel L. Jackson (1948-), actor; Morehouse College, c. 1970s.

- Charles S. Johnson (1893-1956), sociologist, first African-American president of' Fisk University; Virginia Union University, 1917.

- James Weldon Johnson (1871-1938), poet-lyricist and co-author of "Lift Every Voice and Sing," the Negro National Anthem; [Clark] Atlanta University, 1894.

- Barbara Jordan (1936-1996), former Congresswoman; Texas Southern University, 1956.

- Tom Joyner (1951-), host of *The Tom Joyner Morning Show,* a nationally syndicated radio talk show; Tuskegee University.

- Sharon Pratt Kelly (1944-), former Washington, D.C. mayor; Howard University, 1965.

- Martin Luther King, Jr. (1929-1968), Civil Rights Activist; Morehouse College, 1948.

- Spike Lee (1957-), film director, actor; Morehouse College, 1979.

- Brian McKnight (1969-), singer; attended Oakwood College.

- Ronald E. McNair (1950-1986), astronaut; North Carolina A&T University, 1971.

- Branford Marsalis (1960-), jazz musician; attended Southern University from 1978-1979.

- Thurgood Marshall (1908-1993), First African-American Supreme Court Justice; Lincoln University in Pennsylvania, 1930 and Howard University, 1933.

- Kweisi Mfume (1948-), Congressional Black Caucus Chairman, 103rd Congress, present President and CEO of the NAACP; Morgan State University, 1976.

- Toni Morrison (1931-), Nobel Laureate and Pulitzer Prize author; Howard University, 1953.

- Hazel O'Leary (1937-), Secretary of Energy, First Clinton Administration; Fisk University, 1959.

- Rosa Parks (1913-), Civil Rights Activist; attended Alabama State University.

- Walter Payton (1954-1999), former Chicago Bears Running Back, business executive; Jackson State University, 1975.

- Leontyne Price (1927-), opera singer; Central State University, 1949.

- Phylicia Rashad (1948-), actress; Howard University, 1970.

- Tim Reid (1944-), actor; Norfolk State University, 1968.

- Lionel Richie (1950-), singer; Tuskegee University, 1974.

- Esther Rolle (1920-1998), actress; attended Spelman College.

- Carl Rowan (1925-), journalist; attended Tennessee State University from 1942-1943.

- Wilma Rudolph (1940-1994), Olympian and track athlete; Tennessee State University, 1963.

- Louis Sullivan (1933-), former Secretary of Health and Human Services; Morehouse College, 1954.

- Take Six (various birth dates), a cappella gospel group; Oakwood College.

- Alice Walker (1944-), author of *The Color Purple*; attended Spelman College from 1961-1963.

- Booker T. Washington (1856-1915), educator and founder of Tuskegee University; Hampton University, 1875.

- Walter F. White (1893-1955), NAACP leader; [Clark] Atlanta University, 1916.

- Douglas Wilder (1931-), former Virginia governor; Virginia Union University, 1951 and Howard University, 1959.

- Nancy Wilson (1937-), jazz singer; attended Central State University from 1955-1956.

- Oprah Winfrey (1954-), talk show host, actress; Tennessee State University, 1987.

- Andrew Young, Jr. (1932-), former Atlanta mayor and former United Nations Ambassador; Howard University, 1955.

- Whitney Young (1922-1971), Urban League leader; Kentucky State University, 1941.

Sources: "**The Historically Black Colleges and Universities: A Future**" **58; United States Air Force 3, 4; Whitaker 129; Smith and Samuels 55; NAFEO Alumni Record 39;** *Contemporary Black Biograpy, The*

African-American Almanac; *Who's Who Among Black Americans*; *Notable Black American Women*; *Armadillo's WWW Server, Brian Mcknight website, Take Six website.*

Table 1: Fall 1992 Enrollment and Employment at Middle Tennessee State University and Tennessee State University in Actual Numbers and Percentages		
	MTSU (Majority)	TSU (HBCU)
*Undergraduates		
*Total	15,011	6,605
*Black	1,525 (10.16%)	4,486 (67.92%)
*White	13,108 (87.3%)	1,927 (29.1%)
*Other	378 (12.5%)	192 (2.9%)
*1995-96 other race objective	12.13%	50%
*Administration		
*Total	52	40
*Black	9 (17.31%)	26 (65%)
*White	42 (80.8%)	14 (35%)
*Other	1 (1.9%)	0 (0%)
*1995-96 other race objective	12.6%	50%
*Faculty		
*Total	634	325
*Black	45 (7.1%)	158 (48.62%)
*White	561 (88.4%)	140 (43%)
*Other	28 (4.4%)	27 (8.3%)
*1995-96 other race objective	4.6%	51%

Source: Tennessee Higher Education Commission et al. Table 1.

Table 2: Progress Towards Achieving Undergraduate Enrollment for Tennessee's Public Universities, 1992 Percentages and 1995-1996 Objectives in Percentages		
	Other Race 1992	Other Race Objectives 1995-96
*Austin Peay State University	20.56%	17.53%
*East Tennessee State University	3.71	3.40
*Memphis State University	21.41	36.95
*Middle Tennessee State University	10.16	12.13
*Tennessee State University	29.17 (white)	50.00
*Tennessee Technological University	3.35	6.49
*University of Tennessee Chattanooga	10.69	16.20
*University of Tennessee Knoxville	5.39	11.20
*University of Tennessee Martin	16.11	17.00
*University of Tennessee Memphis	14.49	15.33

Source: Tennessee Higher Education Commission et al. Table 5.

Tables 1 and 2 show that Tennessee State University has the most stringent requirements out of all the universities. None of the other institutions have 1995-1996 objectives of 50 percent. According to the figures in Table 1, Tennessee State's undergraduate enrollment is 32 percent other race and the faculty, at 51 percent other race, meets the 1995-1996 objective. However, Tennessee State has a little way to go before achieving the goal for administrators. Also, Table 1 shows that Middle Tennessee State University has exceeded its objectives. And, for the most part, Tennessee State University appears to be more integrated than the other state universities. That is, there are more other race people in the undergraduate population, administration, and faculty.

Table 3: 1992 Black Faculty at University of Tennessee Institutions and the 1995-1996 Other Race Objectives in Percentages and Actual Numbers

	1992	1995-1996
*University of Tennessee Chattanooga	5.3% (15 total)	4.9%
*University of Tennessee Knoxville	4.17% (48 total)	3.20%
*University of Tennessee Martin	4.07% (10 total)	2.0%
*University of Tennessee Memphis	5.09% (32 total)	5.2%

Source: Tennessee Higher Education Commission et al., University of Tennessee 10-11.

Table 4: Black Faculty Employment at Five of Tennessee's State Institutions, 1993 Percentages

*Austin Peay State University	5.86%
*Memphis State University	5.47%
*Middle Tennessee State University	6.93%
*Tennessee State University	47.08%
*University of Tennessee Chattanooga	5.59%

Source: Memo on 1993 Desegregation Progress Report, May 16, 1994.

Table 5: Bachelor's Degrees Awarded to Undergraduates at Four Public Tennessee Institutions for 1991-1992 and 1992-1993 in Actual Numbers And Percentages		
	1991-1992	**1992-1993**
Austin Peay State University		
Total	607	694
Black	71 (11.70%)	84 (12.10%)
White	523 (86.16%)	588 (84.73%)
Other	13 (2.14%)	22 (3.17%)
Memphis State University		
Total	2,046	2,091
Black	318 (15.54%)	310 (14.83%)
White	1,674 (81.82%)	1,725 (82.50%)
Other	54 (2.63%)	56 (2.68%)
Middle Tennessee State University		
Total	1,831	2,032
Black	117 (6.39%)	127 (6.25%)
White	1,679 (91.70%)	1,865 (91.78%)
Other	35 (1.91%)	40 (1.97%)
Tennessee State University		
Total	571	633
Black	394 (69%)	453 (71.56%)
White	158 (27.67%)	144 (22.74%)
Other	19 (3.33%)	36 (5.69%)

Sources: Tennessee Higher Education Commission et al. Table 9; Memo on 1993 Desegregation Progress Report, May 16, 1994.

Although Tennessee State does not produce higher black graduate numbers than the other state schools combined, it does produce higher black graduate percentages.

Appendix D
Original Proposals by Plaintiffs and State Board (*U.S. v. Fordice*)

Plaintiffs' Plan

I. Key Proposals
    A. Keep HBCUs open and five majority institutions as well, but "strip" white schools of their strong academic programs. For example, establish a law school at Jackson State University so that Jackson State can compete with the University of Mississippi, Mississippi State University, and the University of Southern Mississippi.
    B. Requesting a separate board, other than the State College Board, to oversee HBCUs.

II. Program Shifts
    A. Jackson State University will receive some programs from the majority institutions.
        1. Medical school, nursing, and allied health programs will be transferred from the University of Mississippi.
        2. Architecture program will be transferred from Mississippi State.
        3. Undergraduate engineering will be transferred from the University of Mississippi.
        4. Graduate program in Social Work will be transferred from the University of Southern Mississippi.
    B. Alcorn State University
        1. Will gain some agricultural programs, all technology programs, and one-half of computer science programs from Mississippi State.
    C. Mississippi Valley State University
        1. Will gain the criminal justice and nursing programs from Delta State.

III. Admissions Changes
    A. Open enrollment at Alcorn, Delta State, Mississippi Valley, and Mississippi University for Women. Criteria: Minimum of 10 on the ACT and high school diploma.
    B. Higher standards for Mississippi State, University of Southern Mississippi, University of Mississippi, and Jackson State.
    C. Five-year period -- Professional programs will reserve certain percentage of seats for HBCU graduates.

IV. Building Needs
    A. 40 percent of state funds would go to three HBCUs for 10-year period.
    B. Building fund at Jackson State -- renovation of dormitories and other buildings, and the construction of new buildings, including a conference and banquet complex.

V. Staffing
    A. For 10-year period, African-American HBCU professors will be given preference in

faculty and administrative positions at majority schools.

State Board's Plan

I. Key Proposals
    A. Mississippi State University, the University of Mississippi, and the University of Southern Mississippi will remain comprehensive universities.
    B. Jackson State University will have an "enhanced urban mission."
    C. Alcorn State and Delta State will have undergraduate and limited graduate programs.
    D. Mississippi University for Women will merge with Mississippi State.
    E. Mississippi Valley closes and students transfer to Delta Valley State (45 miles away).

II. Admissions Policies
    A. Will now be based primarily on high school grade point averages, but ACT scores will still be taken into account.
    B. More money will be given to remedial programming.
    C. New changes will be effective in the summer of 1995.

Source: Hawkins, "A Quest" 12-13.

Appendix E
Interview Questions

Alumni Affairs/Relations, University Relations, and Student Government Association

1. What is and has been the purpose of historically black colleges and universities (HBCUs) in the scheme of higher education and the education of African Americans?

2. Do you see a distinction between integration and desegregation? If so, what is it?

3. What have been the reactions from the student body, faculty, and alumni in response to desegregation/integration?

4. Do you feel that the financial problems which have beset many public HBCUs is a justifiable reason for implementing desegregation/integration?

5. What is the university doing to respond to such claims, as those stated in the previous question?

6. Will desegregation/integration improve the perceived image -- worthlessness and inferiority -- of many HBCUs?

7. Presently, what would you say are your school's weaknesses? Strengths?

8. What is the image that you want conveyed about HBCUs and your school?

9. Do you fear that HBCUs will eventually lose their identity and hopes for a future if desegregation/integration becomes the norm?

10. In your opinion, will accepting diversity and accommodating non-black students sacrifice the nurturing qualities and teaching methods unique to HBCUs? Why or why not?

11. Does integration threaten the ability of African Americans to control their institutions and educational destiny?

12. Since the courts have ruled in many cases there must be desegregation/integration, what positive outcomes do you foresee?

13. Will desegregation/integration improve educational opportunities and facilities? If so, how?

14. How do you feel about the statement that HBCUs don't discriminate?

15. Should HBCUs be forced to institute and maintain a "quota" system -- certain percentages of minorities? Why or why not?

16. Should predominantly white institutions be forced to institute and maintain a "quota" system as well? Why or why not?

17. In your opinion, is it easier for historically white institutions to recruit and retain African Americans than it is for HBCUs to recruit and retain whites? Why or why not?

18. When did desegregation become an issue for this university?

19. Have there been any efforts to develop survival strategies/plans as an HBCU?

20. What role does your department play overall in the university and within implementing any survival strategies?

21. If there are survival strategies, are students, alumni, and faculty actively involved in the implementation and planning process? Is there any white involvement in the alumni association? [Second question only asked to alumni representatives.]

University Relations (Public Relations)

22. What public relations tactics are being used to help students, alumni, and faculty deal with desegregation/integration and in some cases, mergers or closures?

23. What strategies will be or have been used to recruit non-blacks (whites)?**

24. What methods will be or have been used to retain these students?**

25. Do these methods differ for recruiting and retaining African Americans? If so, how?

26. What, if anything, can be done legally to stop the proposed mergers or closures?

27. Does this university rely on proactive or reactive planning/survival strategies?

28. How does administration handle student protests and alumni dissatisfaction in relation to desegregation/integration?

29. During this school year, or the most recent year available, how many students graduated and what were the predominant majors?**

30. During this school year, or the most recent year available, what was the undergraduate enrollment?**

31. What are the percentages of students and faculty who are from different ethnic/racial backgrounds during this year, or the most recent available figures?**

32. Have there been any quotas or set goals established by the state? If so, what are the

percentages of students and faculty that must be from different ethnic/racial backgrounds and by when?**

Alumni Relations

33. How have the university relations/alumni relations departments handled the publicity that comes along with desegregation/integration?

34. What is being done to alert the alumni and other organizations (NAACP, Urban League, etc.) about closure or integration?

35. If these groups have been contacted, have they been supportive?

36. At the present time, what is the State College Board's plan regarding closure, merger, or desegregation/integration of the three Mississippi schools? [Only for Mississippi schools]

37. Are there any new developments with the suggested merger at Tennessee State University? [Only for Tennessee State]

Student Government Association

38. What are race relations like on campus?

**NOTE: Questions 23-24 and 29-32 were asked again on a brief questionnaire distributed during the summer of 1997 to update statistical information for the 1996-1997 academic year or the most recent year available.

References (for sources used in the Appendices ONLY)

Books

The African-American Almanac. 6th ed. Ed. Kenneth Estell. Detroit: Gale Research Inc., 1994.

Contemporary Black Biography. Vol. 15. Ed. Shirelle Phelps. Detroit: Gale Research Inc., 1997.

Notable Black American Women. Ed. Jessie Carney Smith. Detroit: Gale Research Inc., 1992.

Roebuck, Julian B., and Komanduri S. Murty. *Historically Black Colleges and Universities: Their Place in American Higher Education.* Westport, CT: Praeger Publishers, 1993.

Who's Who Among Black Americans. 8th ed. Ed. Shirelle Phelps. Detroit: Gale Research Inc., 1994.

_____. 9th ed. Ed. Shirelle Phelps. Detroit: Gale Research Inc., 1996.

Periodicals

Hawkins, B. Denise. "A Quest for Equality." *Black Issues In Higher Education* 5 May 1994: 10-13.

"The Historically Black Colleges and Universities: A Future in the Balance." *Academe* Jan.-Feb. 1995: 49-58.

Smith, Vern, and Allison Samuels. "'Fly Jock' Rides High: A Black Talk Show is at the Top of the Charts." *Newsweek* 23 Feb. 1998: 55.

Whitaker, Charles. "The Lawyer Who Wins $100 Million Damage Suits." *Ebony* Oct. 1987: 127+.

Miscellaneous

"Barbara Jordan Chronology." *Armadillo's WWW Server.* Internet WWW page at: <http://www.rice.edu/armadillo/Texas/chronolgy.html> (last updated 18 Jan. 1996).

"Brian McKnight." Internet WWW page at: <http://www.geocities.com/BourbonStreet/8764/bio.htm> (last updated Jan. 1996).

"The 1993 Desegregation Progress Report." Memo, Middle Tennessee State University. 16 May 1994.

National Association for Equal Opportunity in Higher Education. *Keeping the Doors of Opportunity Open: NAFEO Alumni Record*. Washington: Apr. 1997.

The President's Board of Advisors on Historically Black Colleges and Universities. *A Century of Success: Historically Black Colleges and Universities, America's National Treasure*. 1995-1996 Annual Report. Washington: Sept. 1996.

"Take Six." Internet WWW page at: <http://home.earthlink.net/~ddas/take6.html> (last updated Jan. 1996)

Tennessee Higher Education Commission et al. *The 1992 Desegregation Progress Report*. Tables 1, 5, 9, and The University of Tennessee 10-11. Nashville: 7 May 1993.

United States Air Force. Office of the Under Secretary. *Historically Black Colleges and Universities*. Washington: GPO, Jan. 1994.

About the Author

A native of Dayton, Ohio, Kyra M. Grimes-Robinson received a B.A. in English from Fisk University in 1993 and a M.S. in Journalism from Ohio University in 1995. *No Ways Tired* evolved from her master's thesis. A devoted crusader for the cause of historically black colleges and universities, she has been employed as an Academic Advisor and Sponsored Programs Officer/Grants Writer at Harris-Stowe State College, one of two public historically black colleges in Missouri and the only HBCU in St. Louis. In her spare time, she enjoys listening to gospel music, participating in the Couples' Ministry and other ministries at her church, Omega, and reading African-American periodicals and literature, including her husband's short stories and novels. She and her husband, Chet, currently reside in Dayton, Ohio, where she is the marketing and promotions coordinator for their self-publishing company, Against the Grain Communications.

Other published books by Against the Grain Communications:
Not All Dogs (ISBN: 0-9673208-0-1)
By C. Kelly Robinson
Order at **www.ckellyrobinson.com**, **www.amazon.com**, or your local bookstore.